New York Magazine Editor, Matt Weingarden, says, "… an essential guide to the vagaries of the female way of thinking."

Bob Guiney from ABC's *The Bachelor* jokes, "Had I read this book on relationships before the show maybe I wouldn't still be a bachelor today. This book is full of hilarious dating do's and don'ts."

Richard Florida, Professor of Economic Development at Carnegie Mellon University, and author of the best seller, *The Rise of the Creative Class,* comments, "These four sisters have contributed immensely in making Detroit a "cool" city. Their magnetic charm and energy are infectious."

Fox 2 News' Entertainment Reporter, Lee Thomas, says, "Here's Motown Lowdown's best television advice, packed into a fun, laughable read. The Motown Lowdown always gives more than just one perspective. They are sisters who know about love and relationships through experience. Enjoy and learn."

The Detroit News Managing Editor, Everett J. Mitchell II, says, "This book provides entertaining, provocative and often conflicting advice as each Kozouz sister offers her own unique perspective on the world of dating and relationships. It's the kind of lively dialogue *The Detroit News* readers have come to enjoy."

Music Producer, Al Sutton, states, "The Motown Lowdown is the next hottest thing to come out of Detroit! Passionate and enthusiastic, these girls are great at dishing out advice."

Reham, Rana, Ruba, and Leena Kozouz
on Relationships

ASK SASS | Sisters' Advice, Straight & Savvy

ISBN: 0-9753198-0-9

Copyright © 2004 by Ask SASS, L.L.C.

Published by Ask SASS, L.L.C.

All rights reserved. No part of this book may be reproduced in any manner whatsoever without written permission from the publisher.

We accept no responsibility for any loss, injury, or inconvenience sustained by anyone using this book. The advice given in this book is not given by licensed professionals, rather from life experiences.

For information write to: Ask SASS L.L.C., PO Box 1363, Birmingham, MI 48012.

Book Design & Layout by Dwight Zahringer, Trademark Productions Inc. Detroit.

Printed in the United States of America.

TO ZAK AND RUTH KOZOUZ

*Who provided strong morals, love,
and ethical standards for six children, who are extremely
proud to have them as parents.*

*We are grateful to them and are
humbled by their endless support and belief in us.*

ASK SASS
Sisters' Advice, Straight & Savvy

CONTENTS

1. The Crush
   a. Evil Kitty
   b. A Butterfly Lives Only 10 Days
2. The Pursuit
   a. Two Foxes, One Rabbit
   b. What's Your Sign?
   c. Ask and You Shall Receive
3. Firsts
   a. First Date
   b. First Kiss
   c. First Stray
4. Blow Offs
   a. Who Am I Anyway?
5. Dating 101
   a. Daddy No Bucks
   b. The Cuddle Bunny
   c. Who Killed Lancelot?
   d. Premature
6. Ex-Files
   a. The Baggage Is Back
   b. Rock Star Possessions
7. Meet the Family
   a. Oh, Daddy!
   b. Mrs. Robinson
8. Nothing Good Happens After Midnight
   a. Booty Call
   b. The 2:19 a.m. Call
   c. No Call
9. Under Where?
   a. Whose Thong Is It Anyway?
   b. Going Commando

10. Triple X
    a. Dirty Girl
    b. The Unexpected Pop-Up
    c. Lap Dance Interrupted
11. Pet Peeves
    a. Funkified Fingers
    b. Tippy Toes
12. Jealousy
    a. The Flirt
13. Interoffice
    a. Jingle Bell Rocked
    b. Microphone Mishap
    c. The Boss's Desk
14. Intimacy
    a. Regrets Only
    b. Miss Represented
15. Trust No One
    a. Get a Clue!
    b. Who Be Boo?
    c. Bathroom Buzz Kill
16. Psycho-Stalker
    a. *69
    b. Sleeping with the Enemy
    c. Restraining Order
17. Next Step
    a. Hostile Take Over
    b. So Now What?
18. Tying the Knot or Not?
    a. Venezuelan Vixen in Vegas
    b. Ready Freddy?

PREFACE

It's been said that life is stranger than fiction, especially when it comes to love's trials and tribulations. From the courting highs and lows to the dating do's and don'ts, from a crush to first blush, blow off to break up, we all find ourselves needing and seeking advice.

In the world of make-believe, the scene is played out a dozen times before the director is ultimately happy with the take. Unfortunately, in life, we don't get that many chances to get it right—especially in relationships. The "scenes" in this book reflect the typical escapades and predicaments of singles and couples in the dating arena.

The chapters play out the stages of a relationship from beginning to end, with all the suspense, plot lines, character deviations, and unexpected twists that an action-packed drama depicts. Each scene gets four takes—individual perspectives from advice columnists and sisters: Reham, Rana, Ruba, and Leena Kozouz.

Chapter 1: **The Crush**
Scene: Evil Kitty

I blame the cat. It was entirely his fault. My selfish cat, Hugo, otherwise known as Trampy Toes, romped around my neighborhood all day and night. After living on Ann Street for almost two years, Hugo had well acquainted himself with the neighbors, curling up against their legs in search of excess food and love.

Often, my furry little companion fouled things up for me. Like the time I was preparing for a party and found him lying in the warm breadbasket atop the food table—with the homemade caramel sauce, I had just prepared, covering his whiskers.

Or the cold, winter evening when he curled up with my dirty neighbor. It was around 11 p.m. and I was in my warm, toasty bed when my phone rang.
"Ah, yeah, do you have a gray cat named Hugo?" the man's voice inquired.
I thought about it and realized that Hugo had been gone longer than normal. He usually returned home after a few days to fuel up on food and sleep before heading back on the prowl. "Yes. Why? Do you have him?" I asked.
The man answered, "Yes, and I believe I live right next to you. Would you like to come over and get him?"
I cringed at the thought of trucking outside in the bitter cold to pick up the cat. "That's quite all right. He's an outdoor cat. You can just let him out and he'll find his way home."
The neighbor said he would feel bad doing that because it was 10 below zero and insisted that I come get Hugo.
"I'll be right over," I grudgingly replied as I slammed down the receiver.

I ran outside into the freezing cold with a jacket over my pajamas. I approached my neighbor's apartment door and gave it a few knocks. A slimy-looking man in his early 50s eagerly opened the door. The apartment was glowing with candlelight and a jazz CD was playing. He offered me a glass of wine.

I nervously declined, "That's okay, it's late, and I should get home. Where is Hugo?"
The sketchy neighbor replied that the cat was tired and was lying on the bed, then he led me to the bedroom. I hurriedly scooped up Hugo and left while the cat-pickup artist was asking if we could see each other again.

So by now, you should have a pretty good picture of the kind of cat I'm dealing with here. Well, I've had a crush for ages on a different neighbor who lives across the street. We always waved and smiled at each other when we left for work in the morning, but nothing more than that. He hadn't approached me yet and it was driving me crazy! Every morning, I tried to top the outfit from the previous day in hopes of drawing his attention, but a friendly wave was all I got.

Today, there was a knock at my door, and to my delight, it was my friendly neighbor with my cat. Finally, Hugo has come through for me; I couldn't believe it! I quickly assessed my appearance and concluded that I looked okay. I was wearing a button-down shirt with the biggest push-up, padded bra I owned. It was horribly ugly, but damn, it made my modest "B" cup look like a serious "C."

I eagerly opened the door, walked out onto the porch, and greeted my crush. He blushed and said my cat looked lost and hungry, and thought he should bring him over. I took Hugo into my arms and quickly tried to start a conversation. The cat was squirming around a bit, and I stroked him, trying to calm him down, so I could continue to talk. My neighbor and I chatted for a while and I tried to show that I was really interested, but he just seemed very nervous and would not bite.

What is up, I wondered? Why won't he ask me out? Or even ask for my number? The conversation revealed that he was single, but he quickly drew it to an end, chuckled, and walked away.

Whatever! I should just forget him. With my head held low, I walked inside and went to reward the cat with some catnip, when I caught a glimpse of myself in the mirror. "DAMN IT HUGO!" I screamed causing the cat to fly out of my arms.

The furry feline had undressed me with his trampy toes! There I was, totally exposed, ugly, big, fat bra and all. How long was I standing outside like this, speaking to my crush? How big of a fool did I look? He probably thought I was a hussy, standing there with my chest and grannie bra hanging out. How was I going to get that man after this?

SASS takes *Evil Kitty*

Reham
There's no reason why a woman can't ask a guy out. Put that Evil Kitty to work again. Attach a note to his collar, inviting the object of your affection to dinner. Covertly look for his reaction, then gage your next move.

Rana
My sisters are clueless. There are subtle signs that he likes you. For three months he's cheerfully greeted you in the morning, he intentionally tracked down your cat and personally brought him over. He's obviously interested. Dispose of that padded bra and spice up your lingerie collection in anticipation of your next encounter, kitty or not.

Ruba
If he were interested, he would have made a move by now. Three months have passed, that should be an indicator that the feelings aren't mutual. Besides, how do you redeem yourself after such indecent exposure? Move on to your next crush.

Leena
It's not your place to approach him. It's completely the man's job to ask out the woman. Be patient and wait for him to make the next move. If he's interested, he will make the attempt.

Chapter 1: **The Crush**
Scene: A Butterfly Lives Only 10 Days

Did you know that a butterfly has a life span of about only 10 days? Once transformed into the beautiful winged creature, it has a little more than a week to mate and start the life cycle all over again. Well, that's about the amount of time my friend's dream man lasted.

It started pretty innocently. Her cousin told her that she should meet this guy she knew in New York. My friend, Kathy, was 33 years old and was pretty hard up to get married. In fact, you could say that she was obsessed with finding a man to settle down with. So of course, she jumped at the chance of meeting this man, and they started an email conversation. Their correspondence got pretty racy after just a few days, and they both were convinced that the other was the perfect mate for them.

Soon after, they started talking at length on the phone every night. They emailed each other photos of one another and were discussing a trip to the Big Apple. After six days, he booked her a flight for a weekend jaunt.

"Oh my gosh, what do I bring to sleep in?" she questioned. "Do I go sexy with a tiny tank and some hot shorts? Do I go conservative and bring some silk pjs? Do I go cute with an oversize T-shirt? Help!"
While getting her things in order, I asked, "Are you sure this is a good idea? Wouldn't you rather stay in a hotel?"
"No!" she said. "What better way to get to know him. Plus, it's just for the weekend. It will be over before we know it."
If only she knew how true those words would ring.

I helped her finish packing as she excitedly talked about NYC man, Jason. The next day, she checked in with me before her plane departed, and I wished her luck saying, "You better call me along the way and tell me how it's going!"

"For sure!" and she was off.

Checking up on Kathy, I left several messages, but I didn't hear from her all weekend. She finally got home on Sunday, the 10th day of their brief acquaintance, and said, "It's over."
After their first night together, he came up with excuses to avoid hanging out with her for the remainder of the weekend. She came home with a heavy heart and promised she'd take things slower next time.

However, two weeks later, she was at it again. This time, she met a man at the airport. They, too, started exchanging emails, and she eagerly booked a ticket to fly out to see him in Atlanta. With all the same craziness, she asked, "What do I wear? What do I pack? Should I get my hair done?"
I can't bare to see her go through this again!

SASS takes *A Butterfly Lives Only 10 Days*

Reham
Your friend has built up these relationships so much in her head, that there's no place to go but down. She keeps creating her own fairy tales allowing her imagination to get the best of her. You need to talk your friend back down to reality.

Rana
Kathy feels that she's getting old and she has nothing to lose but time. It's all about the numbers. Her chances of finding a husband are much greater this way. New York was a bust; Atlanta may be too—but good for her for trying. Do not rain on her enthusiasm.

Ruba
Your friend is obsessed with finding a husband. Her desperation is pushing men away. She needs to be happy with herself before she can find comfort in someone else. Tell her to take time to develop a sense of independence. Once that is established, she can proceed to date with the intent to "date," not to "marry." She'll find herself less compulsive and neurotic.

Leena
Society puts so much pressure on women to marry by a certain age. If still single by their mid 30s, they are labeled as spinsters, old hags, or worse. Your friend needs to disconnect from the insensitive societal rhetoric. There is no reason to rush love. Tell her to relax and give herself some time to actually develop a relationship. She needs to spend more time having in-depth conversations and getting to know the person on the phone before sprinting to the airport.

Chapter 2: **The Pursuit**
Scene: Two Foxes, One Rabbit

All of my girlfriends are married, and I recently broke up with my boyfriend, so I've been hard pressed to find friends to go out with until I met Mia. I quickly discovered that Mia didn't have any "real" friends, and she wasn't very close to her family, so she automatically clung to me. Within two short weeks of being introduced, she was calling me three times a day, wanting to be my best friend.

I was flattered, yet a bit reluctant to fall into this new friendship. Mia was very sweet and drop-dead gorgeous, but she had a stigma around town for being a slut. This was not the type of reputation I wanted while trying to find a man. When the two of us went out together we got attention, lots of attention, too much attention. Unfortunately, it was the wrong kind of men giving it: losers, married slime-balls, and hairy greasers. We got them all. They wanted to buy us drinks, they wanted us to join them, and they were being way too aggressive. It was insane. And Mia did nothing to ward it off. She just batted her lashes and smiled, inviting even more trouble.

I must admit, at first, I enjoyed the attention. After being with a boyfriend for so long, I forgot what it was like to get hit on. Then after a while it got old, then creepy, then plain ugly.

I began to notice a pattern in Mia. When we shopped together, she bought all the clothes I did. She wore her hair like mine, wore the same jewelry and even the same perfume. At first I thought it was cute. I was flattered that this stunning woman wanted to be more like me. The copy-cat syndrome, however, soon turned sour when I noticed that she had the same penchant for men.

Any time I pointed a guy out to her that I found attractive, I would find her flirting with him. I talked to her about it on several occasions. I even flat out accused her of going for any man I liked. She said I was overreacting and reading too much into it, but the men definitely responded to her cooing and flirting. She often played innocent, acting as if she did nothing to attract the supposed unsolicited attention. It became so annoying that I finally stopped telling her which men I liked.

This worked for a while, and we were getting along wonderfully. I told her about my ex-boyfriend and confessed that I was still in love with him. I hadn't spoken to Gabe in three weeks, and it was killing me, but Mia definitely filled the temporary void of loneliness. We shopped together, traveled together, and talked all the time. It was a lot of fun—until last night.

Mia and I decided to go to this warehouse party downtown. I swung by her place for drinks beforehand. A few Mojitos later, the taxi dropped us off in a shady part of town. We gave the doorman our names, and he let us in, allowing us to bypass the line that was wrapped around the block. The space was pretty swanky and as we took a look around, my body froze with nervousness and excitement.
"Oh my god, Mia, he's here!" I said as I grabbed her arm.
"Who?"
"Gabe! Don't look, don't look, I don't want it to be too obvious. Who's he with? Is he with a girl?"
Mia hadn't met Gabe yet and responded, "I don't even know which guy you're talking about!"

My heart was racing, and I decided that I was going to approach him. Mia and I went over to him, and thankfully, he was standing with two of his buddies. He smiled and hugged me, and we introduced our friends to each other. We talked for a bit, and I was melting, I hated him, yet I loved him. Why didn't this work? His sentiments reflected mine as he asked, "Why did we always fight? I really miss you." As we were just starting to explore the question, Mia pulled me away from him and led me to the bar.

She started laying into me about how I should make him jealous. She also reminded me that he dumped me and that I shouldn't be talking to him. I decided to take her advice to keep him waiting. We got some more drinks and ran into some friends. Throughout the evening, Gabe and I exchanged glances from across the room. This distraction led me to lose Mia. I soon found her in the restroom where she started ranting about Gabe being controlling and jealous. She stormed out warning me not to go near him.

As I sat there on the chaise, I started to get very angry with Mia's harsh words. I headed back to the bar and stopped dead in my tracks. There, on the dance floor were Mia and Gabe in a full-on body hug, their lips one inch apart from each other. I quickly stormed over to them, remembering why Gabe and I had fought all the time—he was such a player!
"What the hell are you two doing?!" I screamed at him as I pried them apart. Mia gave me a dirty look and ran off.
"Nothing. I was just telling her to be careful because all these men keep ogling her," he responded.
Ohhhhh. That enraged me even more! "Why did you need to hug her so tightly to caution her?"
"It was nothing. You are overreacting. Please, please, I love you. Don't do this. I thought we were getting along tonight," he pleaded.

I was so furious I left the bar and taxied it home. I know I was drunk, but I also know what I saw—and it left a horrible taste in my mouth.

SASS takes *__Two Foxes, One Rabbit__*

Reham
Ladies, ladies, ladies. Tsk, tsk, tsk. This isn't an MTV Celebrity Death Match. Fighting over a guy! How lame. If you're both always hung up on the same man, let his affections decide who wins.

Rana
Pull a Shannon Daugherty on little Miss Mia and fight her for your man. There is no reason to play nice with someone who has such a blatant disregard for your feelings. Why are you friends with this person?!

Ruba
Confront your biddy girlfriend immediately or this insane behavior will continue. Ask her why she feels the need to dig her claws into your men. The fact that she mimics your every move infers that she harbors serious feelings of jealousy toward you. Discuss her behavior with her before she further jeopardizes your friendship.

Leena
Don't degrade yourself by engaging in such trivial escapades.
You don't need to be with a man who hits on your friends.
Bow out of this predicament. Have more self-respect than your friend and teach her how to behave properly.

Chapter 2: **The Pursuit**
Scene: What's Your Sign?

We're heading downtown for our monthly guys' night out, the five of us crammed into my Dodge. John and Bill duke it out for the last 40-ouncer of Miller before we get into the city.

"Screw you, dude, I bought 'em, this one's mine," says Bill as John tackles him for it, grabs it and slams it.

I yell at the fellas to stop trashing my car as beer is being sprayed all over. I park the car and shove the guys out.

We go up to the bar, and we're psyched to see chicks hanging out of the windows of all three levels of the Beach Club. We walk in, the music is blasting, and there are people dancing everywhere. We head straight to the bar and I buy a couple rounds of shots to loosen us up. After a while, we're starting to feel reeeaaaal good.

Just then, I catch a glimpse of the babe that I've been scoping for a while. She's walking directly toward me, and I am drooling over her amazing bod. I check her out, up and down—from her sexy, black heels to her mini-skirt to her long, curly, sandy-blonde hair. She stops and begins to dance, and as she turns with her arms up in the air, moving to the beat of the music, she looks my way. I gotta have her. I turn to get the guys' attention, but it is obvious that she has already done that.

Throughout the night, she passes a few more times, and each time, I wuss out. She is consuming my every thought, yet I can't bring myself to go up to her. The guys hassle me to talk to her, buying me drink after drink, hoping the liquor will settle my nerves.

About an hour and too many drinks later, she comes toward us. Quick! Think of something! Not a second later, she is there in front of me, slowly starting to pass. "This is it. This is your last chance, idiot," says Bill.

I know it is and don't want to blow it, so I grab her by the arm and look her in the eyes as she smiles. The music is blasting some rap song so loud it's screwing with my head and all that I can muster is, "Ya know, you're a big, fine woman, won't ya back that thing up?"

Silence.

Oh shit, I'm such a tool! I'm speechless in front of her, so I just belt out the lyrics of the song.

She slaps me across the face and storms off, leaving me standing there dumbfounded with my friends pointing, holding their stomachs, and laughing. How will I redeem myself now?

SASS takes *What's Your Sign?*

Reham
You're in a crowded bar—strobes flashing, music pumping, and your friends are watching your every move while you attempt to pick up a hot, new girl. Who wouldn't be intimidated? Good for you for having the nerve to approach her. Her loss. Try your lines on someone new.

Rana
Hey baby, what's your sign? Hey baby, come here often? I've lost my number, can I have yours? Unfortunately, we've been subjected to them all. How base of you to use a pick-up line while trying to capture a woman. No woman cares for this approach. It serves you right for being so cheesy! You've lost this opportunity. There's no redemption now. Let's hope you don't do it again.

Ruba
The combination of too much alcohol, smoke, and loud music makes for a terrible meeting place. Don't go to a bar with the expectation of finding your dream girl. You'll only be disappointed. Instead, set realistic expectations and go with the intent of having a good time. If you meet someone new, consider it an extra bonus.

Leena
Please, practice being a gentleman! You must approach her with a more proper technique. Women deserve that much more. Introduce yourself with confidence and tell her it's a pleasure to meet her. What ever happened to those days of chivalry where a man would kiss a lady on the hand and formally ask her out on a date? Steer your ways to the days of old.

Chapter 2: **The Pursuit**
Scene: Ask and You Shall Receive

Wanted: Polite, 28 to 38-year-old, single, attractive man who knows how to properly ask out a lady. Must have a job, own car, and be able to sweep me off my feet.

This is the kind of advertisement I feel like putting in the newspaper. I don't think it's asking a lot. I just cannot seem to find a decent gentleman who knows how to ask me out. I think it may be something I attract in men that makes them think it is okay to be so nonchalant. A proper lady needs a proper ask—how difficult is that to comprehend?! If it happened just once, I wouldn't mind, but lately, it seems to be the norm. The most recent attempts are as follows:

Thursday morning: I was at the repulsive Secretary of State office renewing my driver's license. I was in line for the usual two hours listening to the half animal, half man behind me salivate at the sight of my derrière in my nicely pressed Bergdorf Goodman suit. I was thoroughly disgusted by the sounds of his excessive breathing and panting over my shoulder.

I then heard his voice say, "Mmmm, Mmmm, Mmmm. I am so hungry. Would you like to join me for some flapjacks? I'm in need of a cute lady such as yourself."

Too mortified and petrified to turn around to acknowledge the offender, I acted like I didn't hear him and pondered whether those words really came out of his mouth.

Then I felt his finger prod my back. "Ma'am, I said, how 'bout we skip this line and get some breakfast?"

Dear Lord, why me?

Tuesday evening: I was in the parking garage elevator on the way down to my car. An attractive man, whom I have seen quite a few times around the mall, squeezed in just as the doors were closing. We were the only people in the elevator, and I was impressed by his expensive looking suit and polished Ferragamos, that is, until he opened his mouth. He said he's noticed me around and was pleased to see my pretty face in the elevator with him.

He added, "I've wanted to meet you for quite some time. Would you like to shoot up the road and get some dinner with me? Hooters has a wing-ding special on Tuesdays."

I laughed thinking he was joking. In all seriousness, he asked me what was so funny and repeated his question. Wing-dings? Hooters? I don't think so.

Friday night: I had no plans. I arrived home and found a message from Paul from my tennis league. I've fancied Paul for quite some time; however, he has never shown much interest in me. We've gone out with the team several times after matches, but he treated me like one of the guys.

I checked my voice mail. "Hey, it's Paul. Going to see The Rock's film at 8:45. Wanted to know if you wanted to go. Call me back."

Considering that he called at 8:30 p.m., I knew I was an afterthought. I was steaming. Nice notice.

All my other lady friends get asked out on nice, romantic, official dates; the man properly picks up the phone, sets a date, and takes them out for a suitable evening. Me? I get asked out for flapjacks, wing-dings, and The Rock.

SASS takes *Ask and You Shall Receive*

Reham
Right or wrong, everyone has their individual approach, and believe it or not, it actually works for some. You, however, are not impressed by these pathetic invitations, so why sit idly by and wait for more? Take control of your love life and take the initiative. There's no reason why you can't properly ask out a guy.

Rana
A lot of people actually prefer the informal ask. This approach does not put so much pressure on the date and creates a more relaxed, natural setting. Consider the tension between two people meeting for the first time over a five-course gourmet meal of caviar and champagne. Many of us would be too concerned with making sure we were using the correct utensil. Formal efforts should be reserved for more intimate situations.

Ruba
Determine why you attract this type of man? Also, consider changing your negative outlook on dating. Once your actions and attitude change, the right suitor will come along.

Leena
Under no circumstances should you accept such offensive offers. If a gentleman is truly interested, he will approach you with a proper ask. Don't lower your standards by accepting these ridiculous offers of courtship. These gluttons surely don't deserve dates. Wait for an offer from a man of decency.

Chapter 3: **Firsts**
Scene: First Date

I'm sitting on the rooftop of the new Los Angeles Standard downtown having a drink I read about called the "French 75," a tasty, yet dangerous mix of gin and champagne. It's a perfect evening, and the sun is about to set. The weather's actually cooled a bit, and the usual haze lingering above the city is beginning to dissipate.

I have on a new red dress that I picked up at Barney's just this afternoon. I can't believe my luck—it was the only one in my size and on sale. I'm feeling great, despite my earlier panic attack fearing the humidity would create a potential hair-frizz catastrophe.

I'm on my first date with a guy I met last week at a party in the Hills to which I almost didn't go.

It was a Friday night. I got home late from work and was completely and utterly exhausted.

I was getting ready to relax when my friend Adam called and said, "Good, you're home. Get ready, I'm on my way over."
Why did I pick up the phone? I barely had a chance to hang up when the doorbell rang. He apparently called from his car, just two minutes away.

"No, no, not again! I am not going, Adam," I said. I would not be lured, tricked, or bribed into attending yet another industry party with the fallacy that I would meet somebody beautiful and famous.

Adam, an "up-and-coming" screenwriter, was perpetually convincing me to go to these soirées to further his career. The problem was, as soon as we entered, Adam was gone for the rest of the evening working the room. In the meantime, I forced conversation with ironically uninteresting entertainment figures—with egos bigger than their hillside freakin' mansions.

Needless to say, Adam was quite persuasive. So there I was at this party, looking quite uninterested as I scoped out the shelves of awards and movie memorabilia at this "somebody's" house. Then I noticed this attractive guy checking me out while slowly making his way over. He smiled, introduced himself, and then was quickly whisked away by the hostess.

I was left standing alone in the corner for quite some time. I had enough and decided to ditch Adam. I was on my way out the door when the same guy grabbed my arm.

"I'm so sorry about that, let me at least walk you to your car," he offered.
"I'm actually looking for a taxi," I replied with a coy smile.
He insisted on driving me home, but then that psycho Hollywood hostess gave me a bitter look and directed him back to the party. "I'm sorry, I guess I need to head back in there, but here's my card. Please call me," he said, giving me a good-bye wink. Then, before leaving, he said he'd love to get together for dinner.

I went home that evening and put his card on my dresser.

The next few weeks passed uneventfully. I contemplated calling my new guy—only to wimp out. I was glad I held out though, because to my surprise, he actually called me. He got my number from Adam. That snake didn't even tell me. He was good for something after all!

So here we are on our first date, and we're off to a wonderful start. We're engrossed in conversation until this gorgeous woman walks by and stares down my date. He returns the passionate look and abruptly excuses himself to use the restroom.

All of a sudden, it hits me. I knew the woman looked familiar—it is the psycho Hollywood Hills hostess. Twenty minutes and a "French 75" later, he's still not back.

ASK "SASS

SASS Takes *First Date*

Reham
A first date should be fun, relaxed, and exciting. There should not be this much drama already; it sounds sketchy. This is a sheer sign of things to come.

Rana
Stop acting like a psycho yourself and just chill. Use this time to freshen up your lipstick. Have another drink and enjoy the setting. If he's not back in 10 more minutes, then bail.

Ruba
Stop making something out of nothing. You are allowing your insecurities to ruin a perfectly good evening. Thus far, he has done everything right to create a memorable and romantic first date. There may be legitimate reasons for his delayed return, so be patient.

Leena
He laid his eyes on another woman, disappeared, and left you waiting. This, my dear, is not a proper first date. On a first date, a man should make a serious effort to put his best foot forward. You need to have some dignity and leave.

Chapter 3: **Firsts**
Scene: First Kiss

I met Liz at Tom and Maria's party a few weeks ago. She walked in, and I instantly made the biggest fool of myself. I don't know what it is with me around beautiful women, but I always manage to make myself look like an idiot.

I was on the deck helping Tom grill. As he went in to grab some burgers, I noticed Liz and she was smokin' and, apparently, so was I! I guess I was staring for so long, I didn't realize that my shirt sleeve had caught fire. You can imagine what transpired from there.

I didn't even recognize my own high-pitched screams as I was flailing my arms in a complete state of pandemonium, attempting to put out the flames. I then accidentally lit the roll of paper towel on fire, which quickly led a burning path down the deck. I was in a complete panic, screaming and jumping until Maria took control of the situation, grabbed my fire arm, and dunked it into the cooler. Simultaneously, a sense of relief and embarrassment came over me. Liz had seen the whole thing. So why she even agreed to go out with me after that, I'm not quite sure.

We're on our first date. Thankfully, I haven't lit anything on fire, and we seem to be hitting it off. The conversation is great, and her body language says she's into me. She keeps touching my hand, flipping her hair, and laughing at all my lame stories. She wipes the sauce from my chin after I take a bite of her seafood pasta. It was so hot! We order a second bottle of wine as her giddiness and affection are now in full throttle. We were planning on a late-night movie after dinner, but judging by the progress we've made, I suggest we skip the flick, hoping she'll ask me back to her place. I assume that's the game plan since it's only 10:30 p.m.

We pull into her driveway, and I anxiously undo my seatbelt. There's an awkward hesitation as I await my invitation. No invite! Okay, maybe she wants to take it slow. No problem. I can do that. She has her hand on my knee and her head delicately leaning on the headrest as she's looking into my eyes.

"I had a really nice time," she says. "I'd love to get together again soon."

At this point I realize I'm not going in, so I decide to make my move in the car. All the signals are there and we simultaneously lean in to give each other a good night kiss. As I move toward her, my wet lips pursed and head cocked at a 45-degree angle, I clumsily graze her ear with my tongue in anticipation of her warm soft kiss. Apparently, she had a mere hug in mind. As she's embracing me, she's suddenly taken aback by the deposit of saliva in her ear. Oh dear God, what have I done, I'm thinking as I am awkwardly pulling her hair out of my mouth.

SASS takes *First Kiss*

Reham
To kiss or not to kiss. There are no absolutes in dating, especially when it comes to the first kiss. It's all about feeling each other out and I don't mean literally! Next time, try to better interpret the vibe before making your move.

Rana
There is nothing wrong with a little kissy kiss on the first date. According to a recent women's magazine poll, 68% of couples kiss on the first date. Your attempt was fine. It was such a harmless thing; I surely would not fret over it. It's not like you were pulling some Ron Jeremy moves.

Ruba
First dates are always awkward, especially when saying goodbye. Hearts are racing, palms are sweating, and the element of uncertainty often clouds our judgment. She may have wanted to kiss you too but was not sure of your intentions. The more time you spend together, the easier it will get.

Leena
It serves you right to get a mouthful of hair. Save the saliva swapping for when you know a person better. Next time, end a first date with a friendly hug or handshake.

Chapter 3: **Firsts**
Scene: First Stray

"Oh my God! What are you doing? Are you crazy? John is right downstairs!" I excitedly whispered to Kevin.
"I don't care. He's passed out anyhow; he's not getting up. And he's crazy for not being up here with you!" Kevin responded while pinning my body between my bedroom door and his big, hard, athletic body.
"Just get out, get out, get out! John will be so mad at me. Get out before you get me in trouble." I opened my door, pushed him out and locked it. "There's a pillow and blanket in the hallway closet. You can have the couch," I yelled to him through my locked door.

As I lay in bed with my head spinning, I couldn't deny the fact that I definitely thought Kevin, John's best friend since kindergarten, was fine. Jeez, I had no idea our innocent flirting would have led to this type of betrayal.

During the two months that John and I have been dating, he has mentioned his best friend numerous times. They sail together, bike together, and recently Kevin helped John with an addition on his new house. However, I hadn't met Kevin until that night, and I have to say, since the moment I saw him, I couldn't keep my eyes off him.

My girlfriend, Michelle, and I met at John's house for a mellow evening on the deck with a few cocktails. He invited his brother and Kevin over to join us. Michelle and I mixed some drinks and gathered in the backyard.

A while later, a silhouette of a man appeared in the doorway. It was Kevin, standing tall at 6'3", with sandy brown hair, a tan, and an amazing smile. He causally paused in the doorway with a beer in his left hand. An untucked, white T-shirt hugged his muscular chest and his right hand was hidden inside his jean's pocket. He confidently walked over, gave me a semi-wet kiss on the lips, then said, "I've been dying to meet you. I've heard so much about you."

And that was it for me. I was done. My heart felt a little heavy, and I had a tingly sensation in my stomach.

We were having such a good time that we decided to go to the nightclub. The instant we arrived, Michelle was gone. She ran into her ex and was hanging all over him. I had a blast dancing with my man, his brother, and best friend. We all drank and none of us were in any condition to drive, so we took a cab back to my place since it was the closest. We stayed up talking until John and his brother passed out, leaving Kevin and I alone.

Since that night last week, I cannot stop thinking about Kevin, and I find myself constantly asking John about him. "Hey what's Kevin doing tonight? Maybe we should invite him." Frankly, I think John is starting to catch on to my crush.

Worse yet, I now find that every little thing John does annoys me more and more. Up to this point, all John and I have done is kiss a few times. I have tried to move things along at a faster pace, but he says that he respects and likes me so much that he wants to take it slow. Super slow is more like it.

I haven't seen John in a week. He has plans, so I decide to meet up with some friends downtown. As I'm getting ready, I get a call from an unrecognizable number and answer it.
"Hey babe, it's John. What are you doing? We are on our way to China Grill. Can you meet us?" he asks.
"Where are you calling me from and who are you with?" I reply.
Before John can answer, Kevin gets on the phone and says, "Hey baby, I'm dying to see you. Get up to China Grill. We'll be there in 10 minutes."
I calmly say that I will try to make it, hiding my excitement.

In the background John is yelling, "I love you, I love you." Then they hang up the phone. Oh my gosh, what do I do? I haven't seen Kevin since that night he hit on me and I'm dying to see him. This could be really bad. This could also be really good!

"ASK SASS

SASS Takes *__First Stray__*

Reham
You've been seeing John for only two months and already you're undressing his best friend with your eyes. You are obviously not that much into your boyfriend if you're constantly fantasizing about his buddy. However, you need to first end the relationship with your current boyfriend, then wait a few months before you try to spark something up with Kevin.

Rana
What's off limits is often a lot more tantalizing. Your feelings and thoughts are definitely natural, especially if he is as yummy as you describe. You have not crossed the line and have kept Kevin in check. Just enjoy the harmless flirting with Kevin without over analyzing your feelings.

Ruba
You're the type of person who is always searching for the next best thing. You will never be happy with what you have, ultimately driving everyone away. It is apparent that you thrive from the attention of others. Until you resolve these issues, you will never be truly content in a relationship.

Leena
No, way! You are so greedy. You have one man and now you're considering two? You are currently in a relationship which foregoes your right to even lay eyes on another man. You better tame yourself and your wild emotions before your decent man dumps you.

Chapter 4: **Blow Offs**
Scene: Who Am I Anyway?

I was a 29-year-old golf pro and on my way to becoming partner at my country club. I worked hard and earned a pretty charming life. I toured the world, had a great home in a wealthy neighborhood, drove a classy car, and had all the latest in clothing trends. I had it all, except for a man—until I met Nate.

One sunny Saturday morning four months ago, I ran into Nate in the club dining lounge. I was having my morning oatmeal and looking at my agenda for the day when he sat down next to me with his Western omelet. We've had breakfast together ever since. His eggs complemented my toast, and my raisins brightened his oatmeal. This was what I was waiting for. During our breakfasts I would trade my *USA Today* for his *New York Times*, then we'd take to the golf course. We spent almost every waking minute together, sincerely enjoying each other.

Our time spent together, however, was at the expense of our friends. We had neglected them for months. So last Friday, we went out with a group of his friends, some of which I hadn't met. And, I was sorry to say, some I wish I had never met. You know, the typical players who commented about every woman that passed by. His friends really made me doubt his character.

As we were conversing, one of his friends casually asked me, "How long have you guys been friends?"

I thought that maybe the music masked the "boy/girl" part of the question, so I blew it off.

He prodded further, "So don't you have any hot friends you can hook Nate up with?"

Obviously, this guy had no idea that Nate and I were dating, but I figured Nate would set him straight.

I looked at Nate for a response, and he nudged my shoulder with a little punch and said, "Yeah, don't you have any hot women you could set me up with?"

Ha, ha, funny, I thought. But no setting his friend straight. I then thought back and realized Nate hadn't kissed me once that night. He hadn't held my hand, nor had he introduced me as his girlfriend. How and when did I miss that chapter in our relationship?

ASK SASS

SASS Takes *__Who Am I Anyway?__*

Reham
Had the two of you discussed your relationship at some point, perhaps you wouldn't have been so stupefied when he addressed you as merely his "friend" in public. I understand the fear of premature labeling, but you both need to be on the same page. Communication is imperative; talk to him.

Rana
Give me a break. Do you spend time with each other? Do you care about each other? In your case, it sounds like the answer is yes. Labels are superficial and only needed by insecure people. Have faith and security in the relationship, and stop freaking out over nothing.

Ruba
There are apparent underlying issues here. You need to figure out why he is embarrassed to tell his friends about you. It may not be as blatant as you think. I have friends who don't like to hold hands or kiss each other in front of others. He may simply be uncomfortable displaying affection in public.

Leena
Wake up and realize this is a definite red flag. His friends don't even know that you're his girlfriend after four months of dating. Not to mention, he isn't even trying to fix the situation. How dare he try to blow this off so nonchalantly. I would not tolerate his behavior, and in fact, I would get up and leave.

Chapter 5: **Dating 101**
Scene: Daddy No Bucks

I'm a 36-year-old attorney working at Thompson, Wade, Smith and Associates, P.C., the biggest corporate law firm in the city. I've been there five years and busted my butt to co-chair the firm's second annual national conference on mergers and acquisitions. The old, crusty partners fully trusted me to make them shine in front of all their esteemed colleagues and the national media.

I was determined to do my best. I did nothing but work to get the conference planned for its scheduled summer launch. My social life was non-existent. I was seeing someone, but it eventually fizzled due to my blatant lack of effort.

Ironically, the assignment introduced me to someone new. I was stuck working with Jonathon, the planning chair for the conference. Over the course of five months we got to know each other very well. We were swamped but still enjoyed working with one another.

I'm not sure why I never noticed him before. Was I that much of a workhorse? He's quite distinguished looking—dark and handsome, in an exotic sort of way. He is polite, funny, nice, and was right under my nose for years.

The conference finally came and went without a hitch. It was a great success, and Jonathon and I were rewarded with a hefty bonus. Jonathon thought we should celebrate and asked me out to dinner. Not a late-night, order-in pizza while working on coordinating schedules date. Not a Chinese take-out while developing materials date. This was the real deal.

I spent all day primping for dinner at Bistro 55. I heard all about this upscale, trendy, new French restaurant and was excited to finally dine there. When we arrived, I was instantly impressed. A lily garden, chandeliers, velvet drapes, an indoor champagne waterfall, it was everything I read about and more. The maitre d' escorted us to a garden terrace table. We sat above the city lights and underneath a starlit sky. I listened intently as Jonathon ordered course after course, wine and champagne—and all in French. I had no idea that he spoke French. It was then, when I realized I was blushing, that I was smitten. I was surprised we had so much to talk about at dinner. I was nervous when the conference ended, worried that we'd have little else in common. Nothing could have been further from the truth—we drank, dined, and talked for over four hours.

As things began to wind down, I became anxious for the waiter to bring the bill. It's always a bit awkward on a date when the bill comes. Usually, I at least make an attempt to pay. I felt bad because I was sure the bill was huge, considering how much Jonathon ordered. The check arrived, and I made my feeble offer to pick it up. "Let me get it," I said, ready to rescind. I couldn't believe his response.
"Okay, that would be great," he said and handed me the bill.
"Uh, oh, okay," I said half-shocked as I fumbled around for my purse.
Now don't get me wrong. I have no problem treating a guy or paying my share, but HE asked me out, and HE ordered the entire menu! I begrudgingly laid my American Express down and paid for the $375 dinner tab. He walked me to my car, gave me a hug, and we called it a night. I forced out a smile, got into my car, and waved good-bye.

ASK SASS

SASS Takes **_Daddy No Bucks_**

Reham
If you like this guy, don't make any assumptions based on one dinner. There is nothing wrong with a woman paying or splitting the bill once in a while. Wait and see what the payment pattern is before making any character judgments.

Rana
What's the big deal? You just got a nice bonus check, think of it as rewarding yourself. Although women still make only $.70 on the dollar compared to men, there's no reason why a woman shouldn't treat a man to dinner. Relish the great meal, wine, and conversation. Next time don't put out a fake offer if you're going to make such a fuss about it.

Ruba
Over the course of those four hours, I fear this man may have changed his tune about you. If he liked you, it would only be natural for him to try to impress you. Think back and analyze what you may have said or done that turned him off.

Leena
Dating etiquette dictates that the person doing the asking should do the paying. It's definitely the man's role to pay, especially on a first date. I like the man to take the lead. After taking the liberty of ordering the entire menu, how dare that cheapy stiff you with such an expensive tab. I think this is a definite turn-off.

Chapter 5: **Dating 101**
Scene: The Cuddle Bunny

My arm went numb 45 minutes ago. I have a tweak in my lower back, and my neck is beginning to ache. I have a load on my chest, and I'm beginning to get to the next level of annoyed. I'm getting angry! It's 12:05 a.m. I can't roll over, I can't stretch out and I can't sleep! My boyfriend of six weeks fell asleep on the couch while we were watching *How to Lose a Guy in 10 Days*. He has his arm across my chest, his legs are intertwined with mine, and he's breathing heavily. He's the Rock of Gibraltar. Nothing will wake him.

I met him on a Saturday afternoon over coffee at the bookstore on Main Street. I noticed him because of the way he was dressed, a stylish mix of metropolitan chic and Brooks Brothers preppy. He was almost too pretty. I complimented him on his trendy pink Lacoste sweater, which was offset by some rugged jeans, held up by a worn-out, leather belt. He thanked me and offered to split his banana-nut muffin. We carried on a lengthy discussion about Martha Stewart's new homeware collection, the recently remodeled Ralph Lauren store, and several other equally interesting topics. We beamed each other our contact information from our matching handhelds and promised to meet up again.

Six weeks and 13 dates later, I'm starting to get a bit confused. While he's snoring away, I lie awake wondering when we'll move beyond the "cuddle" stage. I have always been against making the first move. I believe that type of stuff should be left up to the man, but I'm beginning to get a little frustrated.

On a couple occasions, I tried to get close enough to kiss and, as my nose started to softly caress his cheek, he automatically nuzzled his face under my chin. What is he, a bear in hibernation? I was so ready to move to the next step, but what if he rejected me? I don't think I could handle that denial. A great guy, well-dressed, and he loves to cuddle? Yet *he* asked *me* out. Am I completely blind?

ASK SASS

SASS Takes *__The Cuddle Bunny__*

Reham
In the world of business, you need to ascertain what you want in order to get it. Why should it be any different in the bedroom? I suggest you talk to Cuddles about getting more than just snuggles.

Rana
What the crackle is Reham talking about? How are having business transactions metaphorically related to the bedroom? This is not the boardroom, it's the bedroom and don't waste anymore time in contract negotiations. If you want it that bad, then make the move, woman! It's been long enough; go for it. If he doesn't reciprocate, then it's time to move on.

Ruba
Don't make assumptions without more information; you'll only end up with misguided conclusions. Maybe he is uncertain of your feelings. Maybe he's insecure or inexperienced. Maybe he wants the moment to be extra special. It could be several factors; give it some more time.

Leena
He is being a responsible, respectable man. Most men would not have even waited two dates before trying to get some action. Honey, you better hold onto this one.

Chapter 5: **Dating 101**
Scene: Who Killed Lancelot?

I haven't had a "real date" since my boyfriend and I broke up six months ago. With no interest in meeting anyone new, I've been staying at home hating men and drowning my sorrows in wine. It was a horrible break up, one of those messy, hurtful ones that everyone dreads, which left me feeling like I was punched in the stomach.

My girlfriends had it with my moping and self-pity and dragged me out to dinner. They were having fun, but I couldn't wait to get back to the sanctum of my bedroom to curl up in bed. I stuck it out through dinner and afterwards, a guy came over to our table and introduced himself to me. He asked us to join him and his friends at the bar for a cocktail. My friends smiled, winked at me, and said we'd be over shortly.

He walked away with the sounds of my friends' immature giggles and whispers. The girls quickly pulled out their makeup and applied some lipstick. We peeked over to where he was standing. His friends were well-dressed and attractive, but I just wasn't in the mood for small talk. I told my friends that I was going to bail out early.
"Oh, no you don't! Stop being such a downer. Come over for at least one drink," they insisted.
"Fine," I said, as I reluctantly walked over with them.

I was actually having fun, and after a few drinks, Glenn asked if he could take me out to dinner next week. I agreed and he took down my information. When I went to leave, he just waved good-bye. I automatically thought, first red flag—he didn't even escort me to the door.

Over the last few days, I found myself thinking that Glenn was a very handsome, successful, nice, and down-to-earth guy. I started to look forward to the date that we set for Friday night. However, he didn't call all week.

It was Thursday and I was a little annoyed. If he doesn't call me by this afternoon, I am not going out with him tomorrow, I adamantly told myself. The day quickly passed and I wondered if he lost my number. I decided to give him until that evening to call. The night melted away, and I checked my phone numerous times to make sure that I hadn't missed any calls. "I refuse to go tomorrow night. I'll show him!" I told my girlfriend who thought I was overreacting.

Finally, Friday afternoon the phone rang and guess who? Glenn! I'm not going to answer, I told myself on the first ring. Third ring. "Hello," I said.
"Hey, it's Glenn."
"Hi, what's up?"
"Just checking on our date for tonight. Where do you wanna meet up?"
Ugh, why am I even going, I wondered. He didn't have a place picked out, he waited until the last minute. And meet up? What was that all about? Why wasn't he picking me up? "Oh, I don't care, wherever," I responded annoyed.
"Okay, cool. How 'bout we meet at Blue Cellars for a bite to eat at 8 p.m., then we'll head downstairs to meet some friends for drinks afterwards?" he asked.
"Okay, that sounds great. I'll meet you there." I couldn't believe my own voice responded so cheerfully. What was I doing? Meet you there! A first date and he invited friends! At least he picked a nice restaurant, I thought, as my mind pondered what to wear.

I got ready quickly and arrived promptly at 8:00 p.m. I was at the hostess stand looking for Glenn, but didn't see him anywhere. I gave the hostess his name, but she said, "No, no one by that name has checked in, nor made a reservation."
"Oh thanks," I said as I turned around. Great, did I get the place wrong?

8:10 p.m. I checked my phone for any missed calls.
8:15 p.m. Glenn finally walked in.

"Hey," he said and gave me a hug.
"Hey," I responded, irritated by his lateness.
"You get our table?" he asked.
"Ah, no, I wasn't sure what name you reserved it under."
"Oh shit, I forgot to make one," he said to the hostess.

Elizabeth, as her name tag depicted, looked at us with an evil smirk underneath her freckles and black rimmed glasses. "It will be at least an hour wait. Have a seat at the bar and I will find you when the table is ready," she said.
We started to make our way to the bar, and I heard Glenn mutter underneath his breath, "Biiiiiiiiitch."

We found two open seats at the bar, I ordered a white wine, and he ordered a beer. Why, oh why, am I here, I wondered. Am I too snooty? Or am I really lowering my standards here? I convinced myself to stick it out to see what would happen.

Glenn told me about his family, his job, and his new house. He was really cute and a great conversationalist. He seemed genuine and nice. We were getting along nicely when the hostess interrupted, "Your table is ready." She sat us at the worst table in the place. When I sat down I noticed that Glenn didn't pull out my chair or wait for me to sit first.

The waiter came by and said, "Good evening, I am Arturo. Would you care for something to drink?"
Glenn responded first. "I'll have a Bud."
I let out a deflated sigh while Glenn didn't even look up from the menu. Arturo gave me a sad look and asked, "And for the lady?" I ordered a Pinot Grigio and told him to keep them coming.

The night continued along these same lines. Glenn ordered his dinner first and chewed with his mouth open. When I excused myself to use the restroom, he didn't stand up. As I was sitting there in the ladies room feeling quite sad, I wondered to myself if this date was even worth finishing. Can I be attracted to someone without manners? Well, I was attracted to someone with impeccable manners but he turned out to be a foul, cheating pig. Can etiquette be taught?

ASK SASS

SASS Takes *Who Killed Lancelot?*

Reham
If you would like to continue to date this man, then you need to address his behavior in such a way that doesn't put him on the defensive. No one likes to be told they are uncouth. Use positive reinforcement to express your concerns. For example, don't harp on him for not pulling out your chair, but instead, be overly enthusiastic about the good things he does. Maybe then he'll get your subtle hints.

Rana
You are who you are. Never go into a relationship thinking you can change the other person. You'll never undo years of personality development in a few dates. Such presumptions will only cause aggravation and stress. Drop Lancelot in search of Prince Charming, remembering that you will kiss several frogs before you meet your prince.

Ruba
I don't want to get on my high horse, but darn it, you're making me go there. You need to base your decisions about a partner on more substantial traits such as; his intelligence, his character, his morals and ethical behavior. You were impressed by your ex's manners but where were his manners when he cheated on you? Stop being such a frivolous little miss uppity and look deeper.

Leena
Chivalry has died and it needs to resurrected. Horrible upbringings, mass media, societal pressures, and the shift toward androgyny have killed the traditional roles that men and women used to have. Where have the manners gone? Most men have no idea how to properly treat a lady, and most women do not act like ladies. This guy is better suited for a beer-swilling, gum-smacking, party girl.

Chapter 5: **Dating 101**
Scene: Premature

I was always against blind dating, but my friend, Steve, insisted that I would instantly dig his girlfriend's friend. I trusted Steve's taste in women; his girlfriend, Carol, was pretty hot, so I agreed to a double date on Thursday night.

Steve and I arrived at Carol's house a little early. Carol answered the door with a quirky smile, and over her shoulder, I saw a gorgeous blonde. Amy was a knockout, and I was instantly relieved and pleasantly surprised to learn that she was my setup.

We were introduced and had instant chemistry. Before we knew it, we were late for our dinner reservation, so we decided to order a pizza. It was so much fun. We sat near the fireplace, sipped hot chocolate, talked, and laughed. It was 2 a.m. when I noticed Carol dozing off and Steve giving me the signal to wrap it up. I asked Amy for her number, hoping we could get together privately. She quickly obliged and I kissed her goodnight.

I called her a couple of days later and asked her out. She enthusiastically accepted and we had another fantastic night. At the end of our date, she invited me to a party she was having the following evening. I thought it would be fun to meet her friends and accepted the invitation.

It was a long day at work, and I was looking forward to unwinding at Amy's house. I pulled up and noticed there were quite a few cars in her driveway and along the street. Amy greeted me at the door with a huge smile and unexpectedly planted a big, fat kiss on my lips. This is going to be a great night I thought to myself. She intertwined her arm in mine and dragged me in to meet her friends. She announced, "Hey, guys, I want you to meet my new boyfriend, Chris."

Boyfriend? Did she say boyfriend? This was only our third date! I felt the blood rush to my face as my jaw dropped.

ASK SASS

SASS takes **_Premature_**

Reham
She's whacked! This is the third date, and she's already calling you her boyfriend. She scares me. Premature is an understatement. She'll be shopping for rings next week. Get out while you can.

Rana
A title is nothing more than that. A title does not dictate how to feel about a person, nor does it bond you to a person. She may just be a bit excited. The reality is that you can direct how fast or slow you'd like the relationship to move.

Ruba
You were obviously blindsided by her comment. Open the lines of communication, and talk to her privately about where you think this relationship is headed. You need to have a mutual understanding.

Leena
Here we go…another one of you commitment phobes. You are into her, and you are excited about seeing her. What exactly is your dilemma? If you like her and enjoy her company, then there is no reason to be freaked out.

Chapter 6: **Ex-Files**
Scene: The Baggage Is Back

It was around 7:00 p.m. on Friday and my new (very hot-blooded) love interest, Nikki, was coming over to hang out for a couple of hours prior to going to work. She was a bartender, super hot, intelligent, and a bit crazy, which I believe added to her allure. Meanwhile, my ex-girlfriend, Jules, had called me earlier in the week to ask if I would be around Friday night because she was in town for an event on Saturday and needed a place to crash. This was her first call to me in a while. She stressed that it was purely a platonic visit and the couch would be fine. Now, I was a little confused at first because her story sounded sketchy, and I wondered why she didn't just go to a hotel, especially considering our difficult break up. I let it go, I guess, deep down, I really wanted to see her again. In a weird sort of way, there is nothing better than an ex, who broke up with you, calling and asking to see you regardless of the "platonic" references.

Jules had really broken my heart a few, short months prior. She had abruptly ended our 18-month relationship when I refused to agree to marry her after she proposed while intoxicated one night. As you can imagine, it was a complicated, emotionally exhausting, very tough breakup. But the fact remained that I longed to see her again. Ironically, after all my calls, pleads, and feverish attempts to revive the relationship had failed, it was my deliberate silence for two months that had produced this unexpected scenario.

Jules told me she would be arriving around 9:00 p.m. This seemed to be unfolding nicely because Nikki had to be at work by that time, so the transition would be perfect. I would be out with my new girlfriend for a couple of hours and back home to meet the ex for a nightcap. I wanted to be up front with Nikki, so I told her the story about Jules (most of the story) and that she would be sleeping on the couch. Nikki wasn't overwhelmingly excited about the idea, but she was cool enough to trust me and at least pretended that she didn't give a shit because we had a good thing going.

Nikki and I met up with my brother and his girlfriend for drinks at a hip place nearby. Nikki must have been feeling pretty passionate, because she would not leave me alone. She was stroking my hair and biting my ear, right in front of my brother and his girlfriend, who were getting a kick out of our behavior. A few rounds later, my brother noticeably ducked his head and kicked me under the table. I thought he was doing it because of Nikki's outward affection, but I was wrong. He spoke to me in Greek and told me that my ex had just walked in. I looked at my watch; it was only 8:15 p.m. This just could not be happening. Of all the places in the world, how could Jules be at this bar?

I had my back to the door, and I really didn't want to turn around. I didn't know what I had to hide, but I still must have had some thoughts of being with her or at least I felt bad that she would see me with another girl.

By this time, my brother's girlfriend, who knew Jules, had caught on to the situation and it became an open discussion at our table. Jules pretended not to see us across the room and sat at the bar in perfect view of our table. She ordered a drink and started making small talk with some guys at the bar. She was like that. If she felt threatened or nervous, she would overcompensate and become extremely extroverted. So now I had my extroverted ex-girlfriend observing my extroverted new girlfriend nibbling on my ear. I hate to admit it, but it was awkward and exciting at the same time. The more Nikki noticed Jules looking over, the more she turned on the heat.

About 15 minutes into this bizarre scene, Jules sent a waitress to our table with a round of drinks for the four of us. The waitress handed me a note with my drink. It was the note I left on my front door, in case I was a little late. It told Jules that I would be home around 9 p.m. and the key was under the side doormat. Jules had written on my note in large red letters: "NO KEY UNDER THE MAT—YOU ASSHOLE!"

I excused myself from Nikki, and headed towards the bar to speak with Jules. I went to give her a hug, and she started shouting and pointing her finger in my face. By that time, she was almost belligerent, calling me all sorts of names in the middle of the crowded restaurant.

She yelled, "How could you do this to me? You knew I was coming to see you tonight and you're out with some other girl. You bastard...we just broke up!"

I couldn't believe what I heard. This was the woman who had ended the relationship with me. This was the same person who put me through hell for no good reason. So, being slightly under the influence and keenly aware that the whole bar was only hearing one side of the story, I just laid into her. I had my forum, and I took advantage of it. I immediately snapped back, reminding Jules that we had broken up because she could not continue the relationship. I reminded her of the "platonic couch" and the "I just need a place to crash" statements, and that we were "no longer a couple."

She called me a pig, told me she was "uncomfortable" sleeping over, and nervously waited for my reaction.

I just said, "Goodnight." I left her standing there and went back to my table to take Nikki to work, leaving the other patrons with a great story for their friends. I thought that would be the last time I would ever see Jules.

In the car, I started the damage control speech with Nikki. She immediately put her hand over my mouth and said she didn't need to hear a word. She gave me a kiss and asked what we were doing tomorrow. Now that's a cool chick!

After dropping Nikki off, I went straight home. I was starting to feel a little bad for Jules, but I just didn't appreciate the guilt trip. Just as I turned on the TV to unwind, there was a knock on the door. It was Jules. She asked if she could come in for a drink and talk a while. She explained that she had arrived at my house earlier than expected and saw my note, but could not find the key, so she decided to get a drink until I returned home. One thing led to another and Jules confessed that seeing me with another woman had really shaken her. She wanted to know if I would reconsider our relationship. My mind was spinning and it wasn't just the Scotch or the Tequila. She put me through three months of emotional agony, frustration, and confusion, and NOW she wanted me because some hot girl was treating me the way I wish she would have.

ASK SASS

SASS Takes *The Baggage Is Back*

Reham
If your current girlfriend has no problem with your situation, then there is nothing to worry about. Keep the lines of communication open with Nikki, and just make sure to respect her feelings and wishes. Your emotions about Jules have been bottled up for quite some time, and you consumed a lot of alcohol. This is not a situation in which to make any rash decisions.

Rana
Easy drunk n' drama. If you have a solid, healthy relationship, then it can sustain any obstacle. An ex is always a challenge in a new relationship. But it sounds like your current relationship is open, loving, and honest, and it can make it through this. I think it's healthy to be friends with your exes.

Ruba
Sounds like you are in denial about your true feelings for your ex. Think about why you stealthily devised a plan to let her into your house while Nikki was at work. Take some time to reflect on your intentions and understand your real motivation.

Leena
Let's face it, men and women cannot truly remain friends with their exes. Having invited Jules to stay over is completely unacceptable. This behavior is disrespectful and degrading to your current girlfriend. You cannot continue to interact with this woman, especially when she had no regard for you. Send her packing my friend, buh-bye!

Chapter 6: **Ex-Files**
Scene: Rock Star Possessions

Being a fashion model in a long-term relationship with a famous rock star, I had a life most women envied.

I started dating Chris a few years ago when he was just in a garage band, playing at his parents' house until all hours of the night. They began performing at local clubs, then started traveling to major cities to appear at bigger venues, where they quickly packed the house. They were in Austin when a record producer spotted them and signed them to a major label.

After the excitement and celebrations died down, I became a bit uneasy about the situation. I knew fame and fortune would bring bra-throwing, hysterical groupies who'd give up anything just to spend one night with a celebrity, but my musician continually reassured me that nothing would ever come between us.

As I expected, Chris and I grew further apart, spending less and less time together. With the star status came endless hours on the road. It seemed like every week he'd be on tour again with his band mates and roadies. I often kissed him farewell as he boarded their tour bus, listening to his beer-guzzling band members screaming like a bunch of rejects. I hated them!

He offered the typical front-row tickets and back-stage passes for me and my friends, but as usual, I declined. As I sadly turned to leave, I considered the idea of canceling my weekend plans to surprise him in Chicago. It was only a five-hour drive. If I left after my show tomorrow, I could be there by 9 p.m. I decided I'd sleep on it that night, but I apparently made up my mind when I got home and started packing.

I threw my suitcase in the car and was excited to start my road trip. After hours of nodding off and several gas station stops, I arrived. I walked into the Ritz Carlton and checked in at the front desk. They had plenty of rooms available, and I was given one on the third floor. After inquiring about Chris' room number, I immediately wrote #721 on my envelope so I wouldn't forget. I began to get giddy at the thought of surprising him, but nervous at the same time. I hoped his friends wouldn't think I was imposing. I couldn't believe that four years had gone by and I hadn't done anything like this.

I headed to my room to take a shower and freshen up. Then, without calling, I made my way to his room. I checked my appearance in the chrome elevator doors as I was heading up to the 7th floor. I knocked on the door, but no one had heard me over the loud music playing inside the suite.

I knocked again, louder this time, and an unfamiliar woman opened the door. She obviously had too much to drink and was having difficulty standing in her five-inch, red leather pumps, so used the wall to support herself. She started to speak, but I quickly tuned her out when I caught a glimpse of a woman seductively walking down the hallway, dragging my boyfriend by his shirt collar. I stood there startled by their suggestive body language. He had no idea I was standing right there in front of him, and before I could protest, they started making out, pushed past the woman in the doorway, and headed toward the bed. Outraged and appalled, I stormed in after them, flicked on the light so he could take a good look at me, slapped him hard across the face, and walked out of the bedroom. "You bastard! You have some serious nerve. I can't believe you!" I yelled as I slammed the door behind me. He didn't even bother to follow.

I hadn't talked to him since that. Weeks passed and I was slowly getting over my infuriating rage. I was so angry at him, at the world, and at myself. I really should have seen it coming. My friends warned me, but I ignored them. My mind still couldn't stop replaying that horrifying image.

I later realized that a lot of my belongings, including my prized Prada stilettos, were still in his apartment. My Gucci handbag, my makeup, my clothes, and all of my CDs! I needed to retrieve my belongings.

I waited one more dreaded week and then decided to call. I got the answering machine and hung up. I called his cell phone, no answer. Countless attempts later, he finally answered.

"What do you want?"

Not even a "hello," I thought. That jerk, he was the one who ruined us! "I want to pick up my things," I dryly replied.

He had the audacity to say, "I don't want to see you. You broke up with me, you don't get your shit back."

Then he hung up the phone! I called back numerous times, and he refused to pick up. Who the hell does he think he is?

ASK SASS

SASS Takes **_Rock Star Possessions_**

Reham
Stop using your Prada stilettos and Gucci handbag as an excuse to talk things out. An ex is an ex for a reason. This cheating skank is history. The sooner you accept that, the quicker you can move on and replenish your wardrobe.

Rana
This rock star sounds like a louse! You forfeited no such rights by breaking up with him. You have the right to your possessions, and if you have to stake out his house or camp there overnight to get them, you surely may do so. You should have no regard for his feelings or thoughts and only care for what you can get out of the relationship, the least of which are your belongings.

Ruba
You may want to think about why he cheated on you. You mentioned that you were not supportive of him and his career. This was the first time in four years you've gone to see him play. Take your mind off your material possessions and think about how you can ensure that your next relationship will not result in such a bitter ending.

Leena
Be the better person here and do not act in a manner that is going to compromise your morals. You don't deserve to be treated with such disrespect, but you shouldn't stoop to such a denigrating level. Moreover, he doesn't warrant a reaction from you. Hopefully, your things will serve as painful reminders to him.

Chapter 7: **Meet the Family**
Scene: Oh, Daddy!

Picture this…the man is 55 years old, balding, and about 40 pounds overweight. He's short—perhaps his excessive smoking has stunted his growth. Moreover, he's a raging alcoholic and belligerent to boot. The man drinks every night and even passes out at the dinner table. This is the man I have the hots for. Oh, and did I mention he's married with three kids—one of which is my boyfriend?

I never thought it could happen to me. I was way into my boyfriend. He brought me around his family a lot, maybe, too much. It turns out that his mother started leaving town often, leaving dad with his son and me. We'd feel bad leaving him alone on the weekends, so we'd invite him to come along.

At first, the friendly banter between dad and me was cute. I was so glad his dad liked me. Then came the kisses on the cheeks, which soon turned into kisses on the lips at greetings and departures. Okay, no big deal, I thought. It's just a warm, friendly greeting.

One night, the three of us were watching a movie. My boyfriend went to make popcorn and Daddy came wobbling across the room to tickle-torture me. Something my boyfriend had pointed out earlier in the evening as one of my weaknesses. Daddy's fingers were all over my body, groping and prying their way into all sorts of inappropriate crevices. His breath, which reeked of too many scotches, was two inches away from my mouth.

My screams of shock, pleasure, and pain brought my boyfriend back to where his dad had me pinned. My angry boyfriend forcibly yanked his dad off me and told him to behave.
I wasn't quite sure how to act around his father after seeing my boyfriend's vehement reaction.

A few evenings later, the three of us were at the casino having some fun, where his dad was at it again. He complimented me on my outfit, my hair, and then ended the evening with a slap on my fanny! Fortunately, my boyfriend did not get a peak at me shooing his hand away.

My predicament, now, is that I cannot stop thinking about this devil. The gall, the nerve, and the confidence he must have to hit on his own son's girlfriend in such a nonchalant way. It's creating a freaky, weird sensation in me and I find myself licking my lips wet in front of him when we're at the family dinner table.

ASK SASS

SASS takes *__Oh, Daddy!__*

Reham

Stop playing dumb! You know what you're doing. You're obviously sending Daddy some signals, which are prompting and reinforcing his behavior. If it's such a problem for you, then stop flirting back. Everyone is bound to catch onto your dirty, little secret sooner or later.

Rana

It's no big deal. It sounds like harmless flirting. I'm sure your excitement and love for your boyfriend has you feeling overly friendly. You haven't crossed any lines, and you are stopping Big Daddy before it gets to be inappropriate. Have fun with your boyfriend and his family, and don't make a dramatic issue of it.

Ruba

You must address this with your boyfriend if you want to continue this relationship. Brainstorm solutions for Daddy's drinking and flirting problems together. You should prompt your boyfriend to consider seeking outside assistance for his father.

Leena

Stop this sick pleasure! There is something seriously wrong with you. I question your motives and character. You and Big Daddy are making some horrible decisions, and your boyfriend is the innocent victim in this twisted love triangle. You both need to stop the seduction and games.

Chapter 7: Meet the Family
Scene: Mrs. Robinson

Doomsday. My girlfriend of four months wants to introduce me to her family. Yesterday, Wendy gave me her neurotic talk. "Wear your nice, black dress pants with your blue, button-down shirt. And make sure you don't wear those tube socks. Put on some nice dress ones. Comb your hair the way I like it, remember how you wore it to Mary's wedding? Yeah, just like that. When we get there, make sure my dad sees you open the door for me. He's real traditional like that. Remember not to slurp your drink. My brother can be pretty weird at times, so don't take all his comments personally. And if my dad mentions Tommy, my ex, just act like the bigger man and blow it off."

For the love of God, could her family really be that bad? She is causing me so much anxiety about this dreaded day that I have no desire to ever meet them. It feels like my first day of kindergarten. All dressed up, wearing what I'm told to wear and I have knots in my stomach, wondering if I'll be accepted.

As I'm cautiously backing out of the driveway, I check my appearance in the rearview mirror one last time. My girlfriend smiles and gives me a firm look of approval.

When we arrive, I do as I'm told. I open the car door. I firmly shake hands with her father and brother. Then I walk into the house and ohhhhhh, mmmmyyyyyy gosh! Her mother is SO HOT! I can't even believe that thought just went through my head!

There we are, hanging out in the family room while her hot mom is preparing dinner. I'm making jokes and the family's laughing. They seem to be interested in what I have to say. Conversation is flowing naturally and easily. It couldn't be going better.

Mom calls us for dinner and as we enter the kitchen, they begin arguing about who will sit next to me. Man, I feel like Brad Pitt with a group of Miss Teens. Eventually, mom gets her way and she sits to my left and her daughter to my right. The food is delicious—a bell pepper salad, asparagus with parmesan, smoked ham, garlic mashed potatoes, homemade butter rolls, and so much more. My appetite is unending. As I reach over for the smoked ham, I feel a tender squeeze on my left knee. At first, I think Wendy is gesturing for me to take it easy on the seconds. Then, as I look at her for approval, I notice that one of her hands is on her fork and the other is holding a napkin and wiping her lips. Well, what the hell? I look down to figure out what is going on and am aghast to see her mother's hand caressing my leg! Oh, my God, oh my God. What kind of sick joke? My girlfriend's mom is hitting on me!

ASK "SASS

SASS takes _Mrs. Robinson_

Reham
I completely disagree with Rana. This is not something you should keep to yourself. You need to talk to your girlfriend about what Hot Mamma served up for you. It's your girlfriend's place to decide how she wants to handle the situation.

Rana
Personally, I wouldn't say a word. Perhaps her mother is just an affectionate person. If you begin to make assumptions and talk about it, you most likely will create unnecessary animosity within the family and blow it out of proportion. Let this go and shift your focus to why you let your woman run your life for you, constantly seeking her approval.

Ruba
Meeting your partner's family for the first time is an opportunity to gain insight and information. A person's upbringing and family have a huge influence on who they are. The fact that the mother is acting in such a manner would raise some concerns about her daughter. What kind of value system can your girlfriend have with a seductress and a flirt as a role model? What types of insecurities does your girlfriend have with a mother who hits on her boyfriend? There are lots of other thoughts that this situation brings to mind. I would pull away from the relationship until you really know the person you are with.

Leena
It looks like Mommy's ready for dinner and hungry for love. This is definitely an uncomfortable situation and needs to be handled tactfully and immediately. Humor is always a good approach. Here's a possible suggestion: you could say, "Could someone please pass the hand on my knee…oops, I mean ham

over to me." I'm sure Mommy Dearest will quickly reassess her actions if she knows you mean business.

Chapter 8: **Nothing Good Happens After Midnight**
Scene: Booty Call

I was out on the town with my girlfriends. We were having an okay time, getting our groove on and in the mood for a bit of excitement. This was when my cell phone turned into a weapon. A weapon of mass destruction.

I whipped it out and said to my friends, "Let's call some men up to meet us!"

"Yes," they agreed.

I started to roll through my phone book at the As. "Should I call Andrew?"

"No, he drives me crazy, he'd be a lot more fun to hang out with if he could just admit he's gay," said Candace.

"Fine. How about Mike?"

"No, he's too artsy and won't want to be at this meat market," replied Jeanne.

I came across my ex's number and contemplated calling for a minute, but quickly bypassed that thought. "Okay how about Dan?" I asked.

"You think his girlfriend will let him hang out with us? She's a psycho, jealous little thing," Jeanne said.

"Ah, yes, but she's out of town. Too bad," I replied while dialing his number. I got Dan on the phone, asked him to join us, and let the girls know that he was on his way.

"Ohhhhh, what about Enrique?" I asked.

Candace replied, "Yeah, I've been dying to check out this guy that you have not stopped talking about. But don't you want to wait for him to ask you out? It's obvious he likes you. Your date went well and you've been emailing for two months now. How did you guys leave things last?"

I explained that I spoke to Enrique last night, and he said some of his friends were in town. He planned to take them downtown, so I doubted they would want to come up to this side of town. "Plus, we have a date planned for tomorrow," I added. I decided to hold off on calling Enrique until a little later. I wanted to see if he'd call me first.

We called a few more friends, and I put away my cell. Dan and Adrian joined us, and before we knew it, we were certifiably drunk. I had missed dinner that night, and after three rounds of drinks and three rounds of shots were forced upon us, I was done. The rest of the evening was a blur. The last thing I remembered was being in the ladies room with Candace, telling her I was upset that Enrique hadn't called me yet.
"Why wouldn't he want his friends to meet me?" I asked her. "We've been sort of dating for two months now and I really like him, but it doesn't seem to be going anywhere!" I demanded answers from her.
"He must really like you and want to take things slow or he could be out with a bunch of hot girls!" she joked.

The next time I was somewhat coherent was Saturday morning when I awoke to the sound of my cell phone vibrating atop my dresser. I crawled out of bed to take a look. Five missed calls and three new messages, it informs me. I checked the time of the first missed call, 1:30 a.m. Oh my gosh, this thing was vibrating all night and I slept right through it. I must have really passed out, so I tried to piece the evening together.

I looked at the incoming calls. 1:30 a.m.: Candace. 1:33 a.m.: Candace. 1:45 a.m.: Jeanne. 1:49 a.m.: Enrique! Oh, my gosh, I was ecstatic! He called me! 9:00 a.m.: Jeanne. I eagerly checked the messages.

"First new message, received at 1:30 a.m. Hey it's me, just wanted to make sure you got home okay, and..." Skip. "Second new message, received at 1:33 a.m. Hey, it's me again, why aren't you..." Skip! "Third new message, received at 1:49 a.m. Hey, Hun, it's me, I got your messages from earlier. Wow! I'm not sure how to take that. That's weird! It sounds like you are pretty drunk. Hmmm, um, not sure what else to say. Okay, bye."

Sweet Jesus! What did I say to him? "Messages?" How many messages did I leave? I checked my outgoing messages: Adrian, Matt. What did I do? As I was swearing off alcohol, I scrolled through the list: Mike, Brian, Dan, Enrique, Enrique, Enrique! I drunk 'n dialed him three times last night!
11:45 p.m., 12:20 p.m., and 1:35 a.m.!

I quickly called Candace and tried to get some info from her, but she knew nothing and didn't remember much herself. I frantically called Jeanne.
"Jeanne! What did I say to Enrique? Why did you let me drunk 'n dial him? Tell me what happened?" I demanded out of my friend.
"Calm down, my head is pounding," she responded. "I don't know, I told you five times not to call him. You were too drunk to listen. You and that darn cell phone, every time you get drunk! Next time just leave it in the car," she said.
"Okay, okay, but do you remember what I said to him? He said I left messages. What did I say?"
Jeanne had no recollection of the messages I left.

Enrique and I made plans earlier in the week to see a movie tonight. What do I say to him today? Do I call him? Will he call me? Do I confess I was drunk and that I don't remember? Do I just play along and act like I was kidding with the messages? How do I approach this black hole of uncertainty that I have created?

ASK *sAss*

SASS takes *Booty Call*

Reham
There is no set of rules for the beginning of a relationship. Everyone has his or her individual approach, style, and expectations. There is no drunk 'n dial rule, so don't feel too bad. I'm sure you're embarrassed. The uncertainty of what you've divulged in your drunken stupor has you feeling uneasy and understandably so. Suck it up, and see where things go from here. If he likes you, this will not deter him.

Rana
The drunk 'n dial is fine. You were just having fun. Who knows what you said, but I would just blow it off and not read so much into it. If you start to fret over it, he will definitely pick up on your insecurity.

Ruba
At this time, your major concern should be your drinking to the point of blackout. Shift your focus from your boy craze to your mental and physical health. If you find yourself in this situation often, then you need to seek help for your substance abuse.

Leena
It serves you right! A classy lady would never inebriate herself to the point of black out. Your future alcohol consumption should be limited to no more than two glasses of sparkling champagne or wine. Furthermore, to phone that late is appalling. Hopefully this will teach you a lesson on proper etiquette. You should be ashamed of yourself.

Chapter 8: **Nothing Good Happens After Midnight**
Scene: The 2:19 a.m. Call

It was a sunny Saturday afternoon, Thomas, my boyfriend of three months, and I were lunching at a sidewalk café. We were cracking up at the new trick Thomas taught the dog, Cocoa. Upon the command of "Shake it," the Shitzu vibrated her little body on all fours to simulate dancing. While laughing in between sandwich bites, my cell phone rang and I answered it. Thomas gave me a dirty look; he thinks it's rude to talk on the phone in front of each other, especially when dining. He never has his cell phone on, nor does he take any calls. I, on the other hand, am on the phone constantly—taking calls from friends and family, and having open conversations gives Thomas insight about who I am.

I wanted to get to know his friends better, so Thursday night we all went out for dinner and drinks. After a great meal, we headed across the street to the Union Square Brewery. The place was packed with university students celebrating the end of midterms, and we quickly lost his friends. Thomas turned on his phone in an attempt to find them, but he couldn't hear over the grungy lead singer's raspy lyrics and the angst strum of guitar stings. We decided to call it a night and headed home.

We went back to my place, walked Cocoa, and were in bed around midnight. We were rudely awakened at 2:19 a.m. by the foreign sound of his phone ringing. Evidently, he forgot to turn it off after leaving the bar. I alarmingly told him to answer, since my first reaction was that it was an emergency. He was hesitant and seemed to purposely take his time getting to the phone. Well, it was too late and the call went to voice mail.

I asked who it was after Thomas checked the caller ID. He said it was Will, one of his buddies from the West Coast, then he apologized for the time. I told him to check the message to see if it was important. He hesitantly checked the voice mail, and I could hear that the voice on the other end was clearly a woman's. He quickly deleted the message before it was even done playing out and turned off the phone.

"Uh, I'm very sorry, Honey, it was nothing really. Just go back to sleep," he said.

"Are you sure that was Will? It didn't sound like him," I responded.

"Yes, Baby, please don't overreact. It was Will. Who else would it be? I'm sorry, Honey, please just forget this. It's late and I'm tired," he said.

I tossed and turned angrily all night, vividly remembering the sound of a woman's voice. Why did he say it was Will? Who was this woman calling in the wee hours of the morning? Unless Will has a high pitch tone, I'm pretty sure it was a female's voice. I was starting to second-guess myself. Could it have been Will? Why would he lie to me?

ASK SASS

SASS takes *The 2:19 a.m. Call*

Reham
Do some subtle investigative work on your own. If you see a pattern developing with these late-night wake-up calls and other "mysterious" contact attempts, you've built your case and have answered your own question. However, you should realize that since you've been dating for only a short time, it may take a little while before all the exes know that your man is no longer on the market.

Rana
Always trust your gut. So many times I didn't trust my gut because I wanted to avoid the truth. You have a weird feeling about his phone always being off because it *is* weird! He's obviously hiding something. Oh, and how coincidental, that the one time he forgets to turn off his phone, he gets a call at two in the morning. He acted funny about it, he was hesitant, and he blatantly lied about who was calling. The man is up to something, get a clue!

Ruba
I would worry that this single episode has driven you into a frenzy. You are obviously insecure about your relationship if you are this suspicious over one phone call. You need to get a handle on your emotions in order to have a healthy relationship.

Leena
Let it go, this is nothing to fret over. Give him the benefit of the doubt. If he's given you no reason to mistrust him, then you mustn't start to question. You cannot automatically relate that one issue to him being unfaithful.

Chapter 8: **Nothing Good Happens After Midnight**
Scene: No Call

I'm dating a man 15 years my junior. At first, I was in total bliss. A man in great shape and in the prime of his life was in love with me! This fine, young thing made me feel energetic and full of life. Gone were my boring, lame days of gardening and reading. I relished our weekend afternoons coaching little league and strolling through the farmer's market.

After a competitive game and a celebration at T.K.'s for root beer floats, he told me he was going out with the guys that night. I have to be honest, I am not a control freak, but it really bothers me when he goes out with his friends, considering they are all young, attractive, single men looking for a little action. After high-fiving the little guys, he ran out with a kiss and promised he wouldn't be out too late.

I decided to savor the evening and time alone. I pampered myself with a glass of wine and cuddled in bed with a good book. Around midnight, I awoke and became annoyed that he had not called yet. I fell back to sleep hoping he was on his way home.

An hour and a half passed and there was still no sign of him. I called his cell phone. At first, it just rang and rang with no answer. Then it went right to voice mail. Great, he turned it off. I started to panic. Did something happen to him? Did he get into a car accident? Why did he turn off his phone?

3:00 a.m. Still no call. My mind was racing with all kinds of delirious thoughts. I contemplated calling his friends, but didn't want to look like a psycho. What do I do? I was in a complete state of disarray.

4:40 a.m. My body needed rest, but my mind was on overdrive, thinking of all the possible scenarios that could have happened. Where was he? I am too old to deal with this crap.

5:24 a.m. My exhausted body finally collapsed and sank into our bed, but only for an hour. I awoke from the sweat dripping down my chest and looked over to his side of the bed. The sheets remained perfect, not even a crease in his pillow. I went from being worried to down right angry.

For the next three hours I paced the room and called him repeatedly. I tried to sleep, but it just wasn't possible. Now it is 8:39 a.m. I hear a car door slam, the front door open, and his footsteps making their way up the stairs. He walks into the room all disheveled, gives me a kiss on the cheek, says, "Hi, Honey," and acts like nothing is wrong. I would never stay out with my friends for that long without as much as a phone call! Who does he think he is coming home at nine in the morning?

ASK SASS

SASS takes _No Call_

Reham
I can't emphasize enough how imperative communication is in a relationship. Express how you feel so he understands that boys' night out doesn't necessarily mean all night out, especially without a phone call. If he doesn't get it after that and pulls another all nighter with no call, I'd throw his butt curbside.

Rana
It was boys' night out; what do you expect? That the guys are going to go to a movie and be home by 9 p.m.? If he does this only once in a while, I would not hyperventilate. If you get angry about it, he will only resent you and pull further away.

Ruba
A few issues are apparent here. First, what type of behavior did you expect from a much younger man? Did you go into this thinking you could change him? Second, you question your self-worth in this relationship by your insecurities with the age difference, and that is not beneficial. The lack of the phone call is a symptom of a bigger problem. Try to identify the real issues.

Leena
What an insensitive jerk! He should have had some decency and made the courtesy call. There's no excuse for this rude behavior, and you need to let it be known that you will not tolerate it. No man in a committed relationship should act in such a manner.

Chapter 9: **Under Where?**
Scene: Whose Thong is it Anyway?

It's Sunday morning, and I'm at my boyfriend's house. We had a crazy night last evening with some friends, so we are getting off to a late start. While he is downstairs making us breakfast, I jump into the shower. As I relax under the hot, running water, I think about how sweet he is to be making us eggs benedict and French toast. I get out of the steamy bathroom and crawl into his comfy, oversized robe. I'm blow-drying my hair and put my brush in the pocket of the robe. When I reach back down to grab the brush, I find a pair of white, thong underwear dangling from the bristles. I inspect the underwear and quickly determine that there is a slight chance they could be mine—yet I have an uneasy feeling that they are not.

Like a mad woman, I rush downstairs and start yelling at him about the thong.
With a bottle of maple syrup in his hand, he says, "Calm down, freak. They're yours!"
"I haven't worn underwear like these in ages, you liar!"
Now, mind you, I am Thong Queen. I have about 100 pairs of thongs in different styles and colors. So he may have me convinced.

He adds, "You left them here a long time ago."
I quickly defend myself. "Well, then why didn't you give them back to me? And why are they hiding away in your bathrobe pocket?"
He replies that he enjoys having them there because they remind him of me.
I feel stupid as he beckons me over for a hug.

I grumpily sit down for breakfast, and I stab at my French toast with my knife and fork. I manage to ignore him by reading the paper and listening to the television. I sit there tossing the situation around in my head, and it is driving me nuts! Are they mine or someone else's? I quickly analyze his recent behavior. He did make an excuse about how he didn't want to go out last Friday, saying he wanted some time alone to relax. He didn't call me all night, which I found peculiar.

Reading an article about the budget deficit, my mind drifts back to the panties, which are my size. So I try to rationalize the situation with an objective viewpoint. There are five standard sizes for women: petite, small, medium, large, and extra large. So there is at least a 20% chance that they are someone else's. The brand is Victoria's Secret and I shop there, so the chances have reduced a bit more—let's say 15%. And his response was quick with no hesitation. But still, what was the deal with last Friday? Why were they in his bathrobe pocket? He was wearing the robe when I came over yesterday. Did he quickly try to scoop up the evidence and hide it away?

ASK SASS

SASS Takes _**Whose Thong Is It Anyway?**_

Reham
There are common signs to a cheating mate. Do you notice significant changes in his physical appearance, his work habits, or his social affairs? Look for signs such as; a complete makeover, a new wardrobe, or a new workout regiment. However, these alone will not convict a man. Team these up with other behaviors such as; making excuses to stay late at the office, taking unexpected business trips, or getting strange calls from people you've never met. Just be cognizant of such indicators, wait it out, and see if you start to notice a pattern developing.

Rana
Thong, tha, tha, tha, thong!!! It doesn't sound like they're yours, Girly. When you start second-guessing yourself in a relationship, that's when you start looking the other way to improper behavior. Your first sign was that you had a weird feeling about his blow off the other evening. Your second sign was that he didn't call all night. This is your third, tha, tha, tha third sign. Throw the panties back at him and tell him to call his other lover, because you're done with this lying two timer.

Ruba
For you to automatically consider the worst implies that you have had some real hang-ups in the past. Have your previous relationships set this tone for you? If that's the case, then past relationships need to remain just there—in the past. New relationships need to start on a clean canvas and conclusions can be rendered only as the picture is drawn.

Leena
Oh, how the mind plays tricks on you. Having 100 pairs of thongs, you simply cannot remember each and every one, especially if they've been crumpled in the pocket of his

bathrobe for some time. If he says they're yours, they're yours. Trust him and stop with the tortuous thoughts.

Chapter 9: Under Where?
Scene: Going Commando

Mr. Commando is a handsome, motivated, family-oriented man. His only problem is that he's too hot, literally. Mr. Commando can't seem to handle the summer's heat too well. His solution…going free-style, claiming more comfort and less irritation.

The problem isn't that small though, it's actually quite the opposite. You see, my boyfriend's "friend" likes to pop out and visit strangers every once in a while. Recently, we were at a barbecue, hanging out with a group of close friends. I was sitting opposite my boyfriend, extremely nervous and fearful of his every move.

Just then, he crossed his left leg over his right, which seemed to happen in slow motion. I felt like a snake charmer drawing a venomous reptile out of its basket. As my cheeks began to burn red, my eyes fearfully darted back and forth in a quick panic to see if anyone else had caught the escape.

I turned my head and saw my sister's bulging eyeballs staring straight at the wiener—and not the one on the grill! As I hid my face in embarrassment, her reaction drew laughs, jokes, and stares from the grill masters. My boyfriend seemed oblivious to the gawking and, wondering what all the excitement was about, asked, "What's all the raucous about? Are those foot-longs on fire?"

ASK SASS

SASS Takes *__Going Commando__*

Reham
No underwear is a definite no-no. No one should be subjected to such unexpected eyefuls. I suggest a trip to the department store for the purchase of some boxers. Present them as a romantic gesture. Work over his ego, telling him how sexy he looks. Hopefully, his free-style will soon be out of style.

Rana
I say let all three be free!!!!

Ruba
He's totally seeking attention and obviously feels the need to show off his goods. His lack of undergarments is not the problem. Rather, the issue at hand is his character and lack of judgment.

Leena
Lasso that raunchy wrangler and tell him that the barbecue fiasco not only embarrassed him, but humiliated you as well. Insist that he dress appropriately so he stops uninvitingly exposing himself to others.

Chapter 10: **Triple X**
Scene: Dirty Girl

It wasn't just another girls' night out. It was the finale, the end of bachelorettehood, the beginning of a life-long commitment, and I was out to celebrate with the women I knew best (or so I thought). My wild sister, soon-to-be sister-in-law, some high school friends and college roommates, one of which to my surprise, joined the festivities of shot-slamming, life-saver sucking, and bar-top dancing. Out of all of us, my ex-roommate was the prudish one, the one who blushed feverishly at the sight of the penis straws and condom-covered veil. I often wondered how she would ever survive her own bachelorette party for she, too, was engaged.

At the club, the music was so loud that I could feel the base pounding in my chest. Young girls were half-dressed, dancing with whomever. Men crowded the bar, ogling the women while shouting lewd comments.

A few too many martinis made my head a little foggy, but I was trying to focus my eyes on what had captured everyone's attention. Two people were completely grinding and making out on the dance floor. They were at it so hard, you couldn't determine whose tongue was whose! The woman's leg was wrapped around the man's waist baring all her pink skirt hid.

A crowd quickly swarmed around and started to cheer them on. The strobe light highlighted their every grope and slurp in slow motion. Just then, a beam projecting off the disco ball hit the dirty girl's hand, accenting her diamond ring and revealing her identity. So there she was, my closest friend, the prude, mashing with a funky Guido with slicked back hair, a pinky ring, and one too many gold chains.

ASK *SASS*

SASS Takes *__Dirty Girl__*

Reham
Wrong, Leena. It is evident that her friend clearly needs assistance. Drag her drunken booty off the dance floor and into the limo before she embarrasses herself and the rest of you any further. Tell her she needs to confess to her fiancé, apologize, and hope that she will be forgiven.

Rana
Your friend obviously had too much to drink and got a little crazy. Strip bars, lap dances, and back room transactions…trust me, much worse things happen at bachelor parties.

Ruba
If she is cheating on her fiancé now, then she definitely is not ready to get married. She needs to reassess her commitment to the institution of marriage, or she will soon find herself signing divorce papers.

Leena
I would not want to be the one to determine whether two people get married. Leave this decision to your friend and don't meddle in other people's personal affairs.

Chapter 10: **Triple X**
Scene: The Unexpected Pop-Up

My live-in boyfriend, Brian, was at work, and it was two in the afternoon on a hot, summer day. The house was in order, so I finally had some time to start preparing for the evening. Our friends, Tim and Lauren, were coming over for dinner at 8 p.m. I decided to go online to find a saucy new recipe to make for the occasion. I love entertaining and I was excited to dazzle our guests with an exotic new dish.

I went to my boyfriend's office and got on the computer. I started to type in www.foodtv.com. I got as far as www.f when the scroll tab came up with the history of "F" sites that had been previously typed. I noticed www.football.com and www.franksnursery.com, then hiding in between the other "F" sites, there was www.f****me.com. I suspiciously clicked on it and up came a pretty graphic porn site. I proceeded through the alphabet in the 'go-to' box, starting with "A." Nothing too perverse came up between "A" and "D." Then I clicked on "E" and www.eurobabez.com came up—yet another porn site. I made it all the way to "W" and www.wifeysworld.com appeared. I was livid! It's real nice that my boyfriend is downstairs "doing work" while I am upstairs in bed waiting for him to join me.

I called him at work…no answer. I paged him…no answer. Ten minutes went by and my blood was boiling! We just got into an argument the night before and he got out of bed and went down to the office. OHHHHHH, was I mad. How many times, I wondered, does he prefer to look at porn instead of cuddling with me. I paged again and again. Finally, 20 minutes later, he called.
I jumped to the phone.
"What is it? I'm swamped at work," he said.
I blurted out angrily, "How often do you check out porn, you fat creeper!"
He defensively retorted, "What are you talking about?"

I told him what my private detective skills had just found.

And he said, "That's not me going there, that stuff just pops up on your computer and you can't shut out of it! This is ridiculous, you are insane! I'm not checking out porn. I'm too busy for this crap. I gotta go!" And he hung up the phone on me!

My blood was past the boiling point. Being a bit computer savvy, I know that stuff does not just "pop up" unless you go to one of those sites first. I took a deep breath and thought, okay well, maybe that was a possibility. I called my friend, Mike, who knows more about that sort of thing.

I asked Mike, "Hey, do porn sites just pop up or stay in your history if you didn't actually go there?"

He confirmed that there are a lot of sites that do pop-ups, but it is more likely that he accidentally went to another site or clicked a link and then the pop-ups appeared. I calmed down a bit and decided to let Brian get away with this excuse.

The situation stayed in the back of my mind while I was busy preparing dinner and getting ready. I started to get a little irritated when it was 7 p.m. and Brian still wasn't home from work. He finally walked in the door about 20 minutes before our guests were scheduled to arrive. My first reaction was to bring up the conversation from that afternoon.

"So you're sure you're not going to those websites?" I asked accusingly.

"You're crazy. Just leave me alone. I've had a rough day. I told you I didn't go there."

"Well who did? The dog?"

"Maybe," he joked.

This made me angrier. "Just tell me if you went there. You don't have to lie about it!"

He called me a psycho and jumped into the shower. I decided to drop it and poured myself a glass of wine. I polished off half of the bottle by the time our friends arrived.

The doorbell rang and I let our guests in. Tim and Lauren were a fun couple—they traveled a lot, so they usually had interesting stories. We finished a fabulous dinner together, and Lauren and I were cleaning up. I could hear my boyfriend and Tim talking in the hallway about their friend, Nick. This 36-year-old divorcé, turned party animal was a very attractive, scorned man who used and abused women.

Brian joked, "Ha, Nick called me the other night and told me to check out this wifey's world web site. That guy is hilarious."

My ears perked up to a very upright position and my boyfriend glanced in my direction.

I said, "What's that, Hun?"

Brian caught the bitter look on my face and said, "Oh nothing, we're just talking about Nick."

I sarcastically added, "Oh, does Nick like eurobabez, too?"

Brian gave me the evil eye, and I just wanted the night to end. I managed to sustain my outrage for the remainder of the evening.

Why wouldn't Brian just tell me? He called me a psycho! He called me crazy! He spends every other night down in that darn office while I am waiting for him in bed. If he lies to me about something as stupid as this, what else does he lie about? Our friends finally left and I was standing in the foyer with my boyfriend. Is this a white lie or are there some serious trust issues here?

ASK SASS

SASS Takes *The Unexpected Pop-Up*

Reham
Curiosity killed the cat, and now, you want to kill your boyfriend. Sex is often a difficult subject for couples to broach. However, you need to discuss the situation with him. Why does he feel the need to do this? Is something missing in your relationship? Try understanding his motivation and work together toward a resolution to this problem.

Rana
Porn is the biggest industry on the web. Everyone's a bit curious. His friend told him to check out a site so he did, big deal. I think you are overreacting. It's not like he slept with another woman!

Ruba
There are many different levels of adult entertainment, each with varying degrees of sexual content. From the occasional peek at an adult magazine and casually perusing the web, to memberships and subscriptions, to engaging in chat room sexual discussions and becoming a regular voyeur through live web cams. Determine the level to which your boyfriend is involved and base your reaction on that.

Leena
Rana, open your eyes here. CNN recently reported that internet promiscuity is the biggest threat to couples. That web-browsing creeper is going straight to hell! Tell him that you don't appreciate his filth and you want him to stop peeping at these x-rated sites.

Chapter 10: **Triple X**
Scene: Lap Dance Interrupted

It was a Thursday night business meeting with my associates, Tom and Steve, and three potential clients our company had flown in. The six of us headed to the Town Grill for dinner. We enjoyed some thick filets and cigars; I was beat down and wanted to call it a night, but I felt compelled to entertain our guests. We tossed around some ideas and agreed on a nightcap at a "Gentlemen's Club"—which is the glorified corporate way of saying "strip club."

Our potential clients were having a great time. We were buying them dances, and the drinks were flowing—until the dreadful moment when a commotion at the entrance abruptly stopped our fun.

We looked over to see Steve's woman flying through the door with the look of a crazed, wild animal. Normally, she was very attractive, but this scene had clearly changed her. It was scary! She was definitely on a warpath. Unfortunately, her timing couldn't have been more incriminating. As a gesture of male bonding, our clients had just bought us a couple of lap dances.

She lunged toward us just as her boyfriend's face was buried in the chest of a well-endowed exotic dancer, who was straddled across his lap. She grabbed him by the back of his hair, yanking his head out of the dancer's shimmying chest, and yelled "Steve" at the top of her lungs. Then she repeatedly hollered, "I can't believe you!" She heatedly grabbed a drink from the closest table and threw it at him. Steve wore a look of utter shock and embarrassment. The five of us sat there in horror as this crazy scene played out at our table. Needless to say, we all sobered up immediately.

Then Steve's girlfriend grabbed him by the ear, pulling him from his seat, and threatened that if he did not leave with her that instant, he should never bother coming home again. With her death grip on his ear, Steve swallowed his pride and followed his girlfriend outside.

Can't a man have some fun?

ASK SASS

SASS Takes *__Lap Dance Interrupted__*

Reham
That woman is crazy! She should have waited to discuss this with him privately rather than jeopardize his career. This circumstance does not warrant public humiliation and is completely unacceptable.

Rana
Men like to watch naked women; it's just the nature of the beast. Women can try to deny it and get angry, or they can face the fact that it is natural and just not a big deal. Men however, should not try to cover up, sneak around or lie about it.

Ruba
The two of them need to work on building trust to move forward with a healthier relationship. What's the real issue at hand? Could it be that he is not giving her enough attention? Or is it that she feels inadequate in satisfying his needs? Most couples will go years without having a true conversation with each other, covering up their inner thoughts and emotions. They need to be open and honest, and keep the communication flowing.

Leena
No committed man has the right to behave in such a manner. That is so inappropriate! She had every right to be appalled by his actions. Any decent woman would have difficulty being intimate with her mate after witnessing such a disturbing image.

Chapter 11: **Pet Peeves**
Scene: Funkified Fingers

Don't even think about touching me with those foul, funky fingers, I thought as I was lying there in bed with the man I've been dating for months. I knew I was right. I had been noticing a pattern for quite some time. I had my ears stretched to the limits, trying to hear whether he was going to wash his hands after using the bathroom. There it was, the flush, the toilet seat came down, pause, no sound of water splashing, and then a quick turn of the bathroom doorknob.

He walked across the room, and I noticed how physically attractive he was. Tall, muscular, and striking, and he didn't even try. Did he think he didn't have to wash just because he was attractive? Like that's a green card to forfeit cleanliness!

He got into bed, leaned over, and kissed me. He started to rub his foot up and down my leg, and I was enjoying the closeness. He took his fingers, his unwashed, just-went-to-the-bathroom fingers, and started caressing my skin—circling the outer edge of my face, going down the bridge of my nose, and then outlining my lips. My lips, for God's sake! I was lying there, biting my tongue, cringing with pleasure and pain.

My mind wandered back to last night at the movies. We were running late to see Quentin Tarantino's latest flick because my boyfriend insisted on washing my car for me. He spent two hours making sure it was clean, inside and out—tending even to the oil around the rims. It was spotless! He was so sweet, always taking such good care of me.

He called me outside to take a look at my shiny, clean car and told me to grab my stuff because the movie was starting in 15 minutes. I hopped in the car, and we sped off for the theater. While he was buying the tickets, I ran up to the concession stand. I had been craving buttery popcorn all day, so I eagerly ordered a large with extra butter.

We grabbed our seats and sat down just as the movie began. As I sipped my Diet Coke and watched the big screen, my eyes caught site of his glistening fingers. He was inhaling the popcorn, and his fingers were dripping with butter. I swear, I saw it in slow motion. He started licking his fingers one by one before reaching in for a double dip—the very fingers that just finished cleaning the oil out of my rims. The movie flashes revealed black, dirty nails and grease on his hands. I wanted to vomit. My hand quickly opened and the handful of popcorn I was holding fell back into the bucket.

He must have seen my ghastly look because he leaned over and whispered in my ear, "What's wrong, Babe?" How could he be so clueless?

ASK SASS

SASS Takes **_Funkified Fingers_**

Reham

There are tactful ways of defunking funkified. A more indirect, nonconfrontational approach can be just as effective. Lead by example. Carry hand sanitizer. Drop subtle hints. Get your own bucket of popcorn. But under no circumstances engage in physical contact with those funkified fingers until they're bacteria free.

Rana

No matter how hard people try, you cannot change a person. Traits that annoy you this early in the relationship will only worsen with time. If you are this bothered by him now, picture the two of you at 70 years of age living in a condo in Florida partaking in 4 p.m. dinner buffets. Can you imagine happily growing old with him?

Ruba

Stop being so nitpicky. He takes care of you and sounds like a good boyfriend otherwise. There's always going to be something that we don't like about our partners. Whether they leave the toilet seat up, chew with their mouth open, or don't tend to trimming their nose hair. Stop searching for Mr. Perfect, because he doesn't exist.

Leena

He is so crass. He needs to "clean" up his act now. Tell him that his lack of hygiene is repulsive to you. Why are people so afraid to communicate their thoughts? If you can't talk to your own partner, then who can you talk to? Open discussions definitely win over the passive-aggressive, evil thoughts you would otherwise have. Give me a break, how badly are his feelings really going to hurt if you insist that he wash his hands?

Chapter 11: **Pet Peeves**
Scene: Tippy Toes

He's 46 and I'm 31, but we look amazing together. He's handsome and tall, standing at 6'2"—a good four inches over me. Our photo is beautifully framed in this week's Society page. We are a very social couple and are at all the charity functions and parties around town.

At last week's children's foundation auction, a few guests questioned why my boyfriend continually stood on his tippy toes throughout the night. I was taken aback as I never noticed this weird phenomenon. I blew off the bizarre conversation until my girlfriend, Deanna, told me that she, too, has witnessed the odd behavior. I decided that I was going to make a point of watching him from across the room next time we were out.

It was Saturday night and we were getting ready to go to the art museum's fund-raising event. I put on a slinky, black dress and some heels. We met up with some friends for dinner, then arrived at the party around 10:30 p.m.

By that time, I had forgotten about "operation tippy toe" and walked across the room to chat with Deanna. My boyfriend went to greet his colleagues. Deanna and I were talking about the doctor she was dating. In mid-sentence she gasped, pointed down at the ground, and said, "Look, there he goes, tippy toes, tippy toes! He's doing it right now." I looked over at my man, and saw his heels off the ground by three fake inches.

While my jaw dropped to the ground, I stared in amazement and wondered how long he could stand there like that without his calves getting sore. His conversation continued while he looked down at the men. They didn't seem to notice. They said good-bye with handshakes, and I watched my man tiptoe over to the bar. He looked around and lowered his heels while ordering the drinks. He noticed a few other people coming over to say hello, and he literally rose to the occasion. There he was again, talking down to his friends. They left and he lowered himself, grabbed the drinks, and walked over to me. He handed me my drink, raised himself, and turned to acknowledge Deanna with a kiss on the cheek. So there he was, standing right in front of me, three inches taller than normal, sipping on his Chivas. What the heck was he "up" to?!

ASK "SASS

SASS takes *__Tippy Toes__*

Reham
Try operant conditioning. Every time Mr. Tippy Toes is reaching for the stars, gently place your hand on his shoulder while exerting pressure until he's back down to earth. Then reward him with a kiss. As ridiculous as it sounds, such positive reinforcement usually works. Nagging and negativity will get you nowhere.

Rana
Can you imagine him tiptoeing down the isle to the altar? My dear, I think you would tiptoe out the back door if you saw that! That's such a weird pet peeve but can certainly be annoying. Determine whether you can accept your ballerina boyfriend.

Ruba
You are only bothered because you are too consumed with what other people think. You admitted that you didn't even notice his behavior, so stop being so shallow. Look at the whole picture. Does this really matter in the bigger scheme of things? It may be just a nervous habit, or it may be that he feels the need to control a situation. Accept him for who he is, tippy toes or not.

Leena
Standing at 6'2" he should not have an issue with his height. The average height of a U.S. male is 5'9" so he's not coming up "short" in that area. Be on the lookout for his next growth spurt and use that opportunity to confront the situation.

Chapter 12: **Jealousy**
Scene: The Flirt

Ginger is definitely marriage material. She does my laundry with care, adding extra softener to each load. She irons my jeans and presses my shirts with heavy starch. She grills up a mean burger and even watches Monday Night Football with me. However, as with everything in life, there's just one thing. She calls herself "outgoing." I call her a big, fat "flirt." I noticed it right when I met her three months ago; I wasn't sure if she was into me or my friend, Lee. Having won her over though, it didn't start bothering me until the day she met my family.

It was my 26th birthday, and we were all going out for dinner to celebrate. I hadn't introduced her to the family yet and was excited to show her off. We arrived at the restaurant and spotted them already seated on the patio—my mother, stepfather, and brother were all there. I pointed them out to Ginger and was immediately floored by her reaction. "Oh my gosh, sweetie!" she gushed. "You didn't tell me your brother was such a fox!" Everyone stood to meet my precious little flirt. Oops, I meant my precious little *gem*!

We sat down for an eternal session of "Ginger 101." They were all drilling her with questions, but she didn't seem to mind. What bothered me, however, was that during the entire conversation, Ginger spoke directly to my brother as if no one else was there.

After what seemed like an hour, our meals were finally served. You'd think Ginger's grilled Atlantic salmon had won a Pulitzer Prize or something with the way she was going on about it. Every bite was so "succulent" as she put it. She tenderly put each delicate piece on her fork and groaned, "Mmmmmm," aiming seductive and suggestive looks toward my brother. I could tell that he began to get a bit uncomfortable. Come on, who wouldn't be with an X-rated dinner show sitting next to their parents? It was like watching "Sex in the City" with your mom and dad right there on the couch. After her fifth bite and the ongoing sex encounter with the salmon, she said to Matt, "You've got to try this!" Then she started to frickin' feed my brother right in front of me off her own fork. I can't take this anymore. Is this ridiculous or what?

ASK SASS

SASS Takes *__The Flirt__*

Reham
You need to have that first dreaded jealousy conversation. Be specific in your argument so she understands your perspective. Openly communicating your concerns will hopefully curb her "fishing" for other men.

Rana
It's your brother for Pete's sake! She's probably very excited to meet your family and trying to win them over with her good looks and charm. Have fun with it. Order a hot-fudge sundae with a cherry on top, and see what she does with dessert! On another note, you sound like a freaky, jealous boyfriend and I don't like.

Ruba
If she is flirting with your brother and getting off on the salmon in front of everyone, then you may want to take a look at your prizewinning fish! She has some underlying desire to always be the center of attention. Observe her behavior on other occasions when you are around mutual friends. This may give you a better idea if this is an isolated event or indicative of her personality.

Leena
If she's acting this improperly now, how will she act when you and your parents are not around? Her actions are utterly tasteless and are a disgrace. You better end the relationship now, before she dumps you for the "catch of the day."

Chapter 13: **Interoffice**
Scene: Jingle Bell Rocked

My boss is a very quirky and eccentric guy. No one at the company knows much about him because he never discusses his personal life. He doesn't even have any pictures of his family in his office. He doesn't fraternize with anyone—except for once a year at our holiday party.

It's that time of year again, and I'm absolutely dreading the boring shindig, it's such a drag. Having been here since I graduated from college nine years ago, it serves as a constant reminder of my stagnant life. Yeah, I had dreams once; I actually thought I'd move to New York or D.C. to work for a large agency. Unfortunately, things don't always work out the way you expect. I'm so bored with the same old faces, same coffee conversations, and same parties.

I look at the clock and realize the party has started 45 minutes ago. I begrudgingly throw on my suit and make my way to the restaurant where our ad agency has their party every year. I arrive only to engage in the obligatory chitchat with my boss and a few others, then I head over to the bar to hang out with my friend, Rami Z. Z, as the graphic designers from the third floor call my funny friend, questions why our freaky boss never brings his wife to the party. We wonder if she's got some physical ailment and he's embarrassed of her. We joke, discussing all the possible scenarios. We continue entertaining ourselves while downing a few more vodka tonics.

I was thinking of calling it a night when a stunning brunette enters the restaurant. "Who the hell is that?" declares Z.
"Perhaps I won't be leaving after all. I'm hooking this up; I'll catch up with you tomorrow." I leave Z and walk right up to her.

I spark up a conversation, and to my surprise, she's actually reciprocating. It's apparent she's had too many drinks, but we order a few more anyway. Before you know it, she's spilling her guts. She begins her sad tale of how her man never takes her anywhere anymore. He used to take her to parties like this one long ago, but now things have fizzled and were just not the same. I lend a shoulder for her to cry on, thinking this was my in. Her hand, then, aggressively makes its way to my knee, and she begins to caress my inner thigh. The conversation progresses, as does our P.D.A.

I quickly realize that we're getting a lot of disapproving stares. I am reviewing the options of the segue to my place…that is until my boss rocks my world with a tap on my shoulder and says, "I see you've met my wife." Where do I go from here?

"ASK SASS

SASS Takes *__Jingle Bell Rocked__*

Reham
The damage is done. There's no sidestepping the scandal. Accept responsibility. Your only chance at redemption is an apology and an explanation to your boss.

Rana
This was not your fault. How were you to know that she was the boss's wife? Ebenezer Scrooge doesn't take the poor woman out, so he should be fortunate that you were merely entertaining her. This problem is not yours. It is an issue between your boss and his wife. Accept no responsibility whatsoever.

Ruba
Politely excuse yourself from the situation as if you have done nothing wrong, then leave. Do not stop along the way to talk to anyone. Chances are everyone else knows you were hitting on the boss's wife and will want to find out what happened. Whatever you do, don't add to the gossip and create more drama. Let your boss make the move by waiting to see how he treats you on Monday.

Leena
Office parties tend to jeopardize careers when people decide to drink too much and make fools of themselves. Employees should be cognizant of the image they display when engaging in such social events. Do you want to be labeled the office drunk or playboy? I think not. So do not mix business with pleasure in future engagements.

Chapter 13: **Interoffice**
Scene: Microphone Mishap

It was 6 a.m. Mark rolled over, gave me a kiss on my forehead, and whispered, "I'll see you this afternoon."

I was half-awake and responded, "Great, good luck" in my groggy morning voice. I dozed off for one more hour and awoke to the buzzing alarm clock that had just interrupted my amazing dream. I quickly reached out, aimlessly tapping the snooze button. My head sank back into the pillow, and I forced myself to continue the dream about an island vacation with some babe. It didn't work. So, annoyed, I got out of bed to start my daily routine.

I arrived at work early to complete an assignment before the afternoon's conference. Unlike all the others, I was actually looking forward to this one. It wasn't so much the content of the conference I was anticipating, but rather the presenter, Mark Turner. The ladies around the office referred to my boyfriend as "eye candy," constantly staring at him, but never daring to get involved with a co-worker. I, on the other hand, didn't allow such nonsense to control my love life. We had been dating for five months and the relationship was really heating up.

I went down to help Mark set up the cordless microphone, clipping it firmly to the lapel of his suit jacket. At a quarter to noon, the staff trickled into the conference room. He began his presentation and received several applauds throughout. Halfway through, snacks and refreshments were carted in, and Mark released everyone for a brief intermission.

A few nicotine addicts scurried outside to the smoking court to get their fix. Most of the others headed to their offices to check their email and voice mail or to take care of small business matters. Well, it was apparent Mark had some "business" of his own to take care of, and it was no "small matter." A few minutes later, *his* business turned out to be everyone's. Mark headed into the men's room and evidently went to war with the egg sandwich he had for breakfast. You'd think that such information should be kept private, but the unfortunate twist was that Mark forgot to turn off his cordless microphone.

The groaning and grunting that penetrated the conference room speakers forever changed his reputation. It's unbelievable how one's decent from "eye candy" to "microphone mishap" can happen in a matter of seconds. He is still unaware of his public announcement, and now, I just cannot look at him in the same light. Every time our relationship starts to get hot, I am haunted by the office jokes and cringe at the thought of being intimate. I don't know what to do.

ASK *SASS*

SASS Takes *Microphone Mishap*

Reham
The poor guy would die of embarrassment if he knew what transpired. The only way to get past this is to blow it off. You'll never be able to sustain a relationship if you harp on such matters. Grow up and realize, if you get married, you're going to share a bathroom with your mate, so stop being so immature about it.

Rana
I can understand the difficulty in being intimate with him after this dirty deed. It's unfortunate, but little things can send us running. Ick, ick, ick. The thought of kissing him would even gross me out. It is challenging to continue on with someone you can no longer respect. Take a break for a few days and see how you feel about him in a little while.

Ruba
It was an honest mistake. If you are so quick to "dump" him after such a trivial thing, what's going to happen when real-life issues and stress enter the picture? I question your ability to be in a meaningful relationship.

Leena
Stand by your man and scold all the petty employees who have nothing better to do than talk about other people's problems. Be the better person, and protect him from the gossip rather than shy away from the embarrassment.

Chapter 13: **Interoffice**
Scene: The Boss's Desk

I work on the top floor of a 40-story building. Our financial services company has branches all over the world with over 6,000 employees. It is a renowned company with plenty of opportunities for advancement. The fringe benefits include corporate trips, game tickets, and concierge services. I adore my colleagues who are primarily fun, young, energetic people with brilliant ideas—but I hate my employer.

The CEO, Simon Muelleroni, is a very attractive man in his late 40s. He immigrated to the United States as a child with his Italian parents. He put himself through school and worked hard to quickly build his company from the ground up. Written up as the city's most eligible bachelor, hundreds of women lined up to date him. However, he soon married a beautiful, supportive woman named Lynn. She cheerfully attends all of our company functions and packs his lunch daily. I respect her continued support for a man who puts in an 80-hour work week.

As Mr. Muelleroni's executive assistant for 5 years, I have developed quite a fondness for Lynn. We shop and chat during my lunch breaks and haven't missed celebrating one birthday, special occasion, or holiday together.

Last week, I had been working overtime, helping Mr. Muelleroni meet a final deadline. The hectic pace had me feeling physically and mentally exhausted. Working in very close quarters, Mr. Muelleroni heard me when I let out a big, stressful sigh. He took that as an opportunity to help me. He started massaging my shoulders and neck, and stroked my hair. I immediately became very uncomfortable and got up from my chair.

He sensed my anxiety and said, "I was just trying to help you relieve some stress."

I didn't want to overreact so I merely replied, "Thank you," and left his office.

Yesterday, he called me in to finalize some documents that were going out for a competitive bid. As I was sorting the papers on his desk, he came up from behind, wrapped his arms around my waist, and pressed his body tightly against mine. I froze. I didn't know what to do. This was my boss! The boss who was married to a wonderful woman—a woman I considered my friend.

ASK SASS

SASS takes *The Boss's Desk*

Reham
You are in a stressful situation, so don't make any rash decisions that could jeopardize your job. Wait it out to see if his actions escalate. His future behavior should dictate your recourse.

Rana
Formalize the complaint by taking it to human resources. You do not need to confront him directly or be obliged to tell his wife. It is not your place. Let the corporate professionals handle the situation. Their documentation will ensure serious repercussions if he persists with further harassment, ultimately protecting your position.

Ruba
You cannot allow his behavior to continue, however you may want to make sure you are not sending out any wrong signals. The fact that you said, "thank you" after the first offense was his opening. Check your hemlines, your blouses, and your behavior to ensure your level of appropriateness before taking action.

Leena
As your good friend, the wife should be privy to this information. Bring it to her attention immediately. Tell her that it makes you uncomfortable and you aren't sure how to approach him. Explain that you fear jeopardizing your position and their relationship. I'm sure she'll appreciate your honesty. If there's anyone she'll be mad at, it will surely be him.

Chapter 14: **Intimacy**
Scene: Regrets Only

"Have you ever fantasized about someone else while you are with me?" I ask my boyfriend, Dave.
"What?" he asks me in complete astonishment.
I repeat my question, this time concentrating very hard on his facial expressions and body language, looking for any sign of a lie.
"No," he replies without hesitation. "Do you?" he asks back.

My body stiffens. I don't really know why. I knew the question would bounce back to me. My mind races frantically to find an acceptable answer. Of course I fantasize about other men. I think of Antonio Banderas, Tom Cruise, and all the other Hollywood hunks. But quite a few times I have had illicit images of John, Dave's best friend. He's a babe, but just recently got married. What's the harm, I think. They are just fantasies.

I realize that Dave is still staring at me, waiting for an answer. He repeats the question with a nervous laugh anticipating my response. "Do you fantasize about other men when we are together?"
"Yes." I smile, trying to lighten the situation.
Immediately, he demands to know who.
Great. Why did I open my big mouth?

I succumb to his pleas. "Guess, and I will tell you if you are right."
"I don't know; just tell me," he says annoyed.
I list my movie-star crushes, and he laughs and lists a few sultry actresses. I am so comfortable with our conversation and the way he plays along that I add John's name. He tenses and says, "John who?"
Shit! I manage to stutter, "Ahhhh, John...Denver."
"It is not," he says. "John who?" he demands once again.

I kiss him on the cheek, trying to change the subject. He knows exactly which John I was referring to, his competition since the fifth grade. The same John who stole his prom date. The very John who made center on the basketball team and football quarterback. Dave gets up from the bed and storms away, saying, "I can't believe you fantasize about my best friend when you're with me! Why don't you just date John?!" Oh jeez, what now?

ASK SASS

SASS Takes **_Regrets Only_**

Reham
John Denver is all you could muster up? What about John Stamos, Jon Bon Jovi, Johnny Depp, or John Travolta? Your major regret should be lack of a better pick. It sounds like your man has to deal with his own insecurities about his competitive friend.

Rana
This is ridiculous; fantasies are just harmless thoughts. It's not like you slept with his friend. Couples should be able to have open, honest communication without feeling threatened or hurt. I want to be able to share everything with my partner. If you have to hide something, then there's something to worry about.

Ruba
It is one thing to have fleeting thoughts about a make-believe love affair, but to have "illicit" images of your boyfriend's best friend is not right. It is not harmless, as Rana says. A thought typically leads to an action, and I don't like where this is headed.

Leena
Generally speaking, sharing thoughts of betrayal will only result in hurt—even if they are just fantasies. There are certain things in life that you should keep to yourself; this is one of them. Start backtracking and spare your partner's feelings.

Chapter 14: **Intimacy**
Scene: Miss Represented

He entered the room pretending to be an exotic dancer, swaying his hips back and forth to the beat of the music. What a sight—an exotic dancer with a hairy chest and big calves. He was such the buffoon, always making me laugh.

Here it was...the big night. We have waited so long for this. Our one-year anniversary and we decided we were ready. The night was perfect. The ambiance was perfect. He was perfect. The breeze was lightly whistling through the window, gently blowing the drapes. The wind chimes outside created a perfect melody and blended smoothly with the sound of the crickets. Scented candles were lit, creating a magnificent glow on the ceiling and walls. The sheets were so fresh and crisp, and the feather bed molded perfectly to the shape of my body. I felt wonderful and excited, yet utterly relaxed.

I turned on my side to get a better view of his dancing. He got on his knees and started to crawl toward me, slowly and cautiously, like a wild tiger. I lightly slapped his shoulder, hinting to shift into serious mode. He got under the sheets and wrapped his arms around me. His fingers touched my cheek, and he slowly began to caress my skin. He propped his head up on one arm and leaned over to give me a light kiss, which left me wanting more. As he was running his fingers through my hair, he looked at me in way that gave me chills. It was such a deep look. It almost made me feel as though we were one. He softly kissed me and whispered, "Let's make love, Sarah."
I slapped him hard across the face and demanded, "Sarah!?! Who the hell is Sarah?"

ASK *SASS*

SASS takes *__Miss Represented__*

Reham
Assuming this is his first slip, everybody's allowed a mulligan. If the behavior continues, then you have a problem.

Rana
You've seriously worked this wild tiger up so much that he doesn't even know your name. His sexual frustration has been pent up for a year; I can understand the slip up. Don't fret over it and carry on with the matter at hand.

Ruba
Explore why you decided to make him wait a year. Have you not trusted him all along? Was he seeing other people? Were you trying to control the relationship by using sex as the tool? Openly discuss your fears and disappointment to come to a higher level of trust.

Leena
He is a buffoon! He ruined this much anticipated moment. Teach him a lesson; make him wait another whole year until he can get your name straight. In the meantime, tell lover boy to come clean about who the heck Sarah is.

Chapter 15: **Trust No One**
Scene: Get a Clue!

I told Sandy to hire a private investigator, but she wouldn't listen. "Just have him followed for a week. Then make your decision," I said. But she just turned her back as if she did not hear me, which is usually what she does when it comes to Bill. Why does she bother to ask for my advice if she never takes it?

Sandy has been with Bill for about three years. I constantly told her that she was wasting her time because rumor had it that he was cheating on her. He was a player from day one, a real smooth talker. He fed her so much bull, weaseling his way out of anything.

Bill's sales job took him out of town weekly and sometimes for long weekends to service his accounts across the United States. I found it odd that he would never tell her where he was staying or when he was coming home. She tried to reach him on his cell, but it was never on. She left him messages, but he rarely called her back. When he did call, it was either very late at night or early in the morning, and he would whisper that he was in a hurry and had to go, never ending the conversation with "I love you."

He never gave her details of his trips and often got his stories mixed up. Once, he recanted a story about a client that he told her the week prior. I could tell something was wrong when she hung up the phone. She acted weird, but never dared to confront him.

One night, when he got back from one of his "meetings," Sandy welcomed him with dinner. While he was in the shower, his cell phone rang. She didn't recognize the number and wanted to know who it was, so she answered the phone. Whomever it was hung up. The phone rang again, teasing Sandy to answer. The voice on the other end was a woman's. "Who's this?" the woman asked.

"Who is *this*?" Sandy demanded back.
"I'm looking for Bill," replied the woman.
"Who did you say this was?"
As soon as she asked the question, Bill walked in and glared at her. He angrily grabbed the cell phone out of her hand, turned it off, and yelled, "Don't ever answer my phone again!"
What is my friend thinking?

ASK SASS

SASS Takes *__Get a Clue!__*

Reham
Advise your friend to wait until he falls asleep and snatch his cell phone. Quickly jot down the mystery caller's number and contact the woman the next day. Your friend may come off as a total idiot and be utterly humiliated, but it is worth the quest for truth.

Rana
Rumors are 99% factual. Your friend needs to wake up and stop looking the other way. I know she doesn't want to believe it, but these signs indicate that he is cheating or acting inappropriately. She shouldn't stick around for another excuse or fake explanation. She needs to find someone who can be in a monogamous relationship.

Ruba
Your friend needs to muster up some self-confidence and confront her boyfriend, or he will continue to take advantage of her. If she doesn't tackle this issue, she will find the same problem arising in future relationships.

Leena
He may be under a lot of pressure at work and, as a result, has been acting differently. Have you considered that he wasn't taking her calls or whispering "I love you" because he was working or in the middle of a business meeting. She assumes he leaves town for pleasure and may have no concept of his professional demands. It is easier to draw these conclusions as an outsider looking in. She needs to trust her man and try relieving his pressure, rather than adding to it.

Chapter 15: **Trust No One**
Scene: Who Be Boo?

Maybe it was just the difficulty I had in trusting people, but I have always been suspicious of my girlfriend. She never really gave me a reason to mistrust her, but it just seemed like she was up to no good. Maybe it was her personality. She was so vain, forever consumed with her appearance. Hours in front of the mirror were matched by the hours she spent on the computer. She called herself a modern day techy, which I never understood why as she was a music instructor. Unless composing her own music, what were her PC needs? She was no Beethoven and her computer "literacy" skills had me even setting up her Yahoo! account.

When I arrived at her house, I must have caught her by surprise, because she was acting out of sorts and was on that damn computer again. I noticed that she quickly closed her email and logged off. We had planned to rent a movie, and it was her turn to pick the flick. I told her I'd wait at the house while she made the short trip to Blockbuster.

As soon as I heard the engine start, I headed to the back room to see what I could find. I logged into Yahoo! and plugged in her username and password without hesitation. Her inbox read "1 new message." I was afraid to click on it because, as soon as I did, she would be suspicious. What if it was nothing? Do I? Do I? My fingers were shaking as I clicked on the "1 new message" link and there it was...

Hi Cutie,
It's great to hear from you again! I can't wait until the next time we can see each other. Email me and let me know what days you have available next week. Miss ya!
☺
XOXO,
Boo

Boo! Who the heck is Boo?

ASK SASS

SASS Takes *Who Be Boo?*

Reham
It's a sneaky suggestion, but a little investigative work can go a long way. She's obviously hiding something, so keep digging. Go through her sent folder and her saved messages, and try to piece this mystery together.

Rana
First of all, Mr. Nosey, you should not be prying around in your woman's inbox. Things in writing seem much more serious than they actually are. I have nicknames for a lot of my friends. You may be overreacting and reading too much into this.

Ruba
You had insecurities with the relationship before the email discovery. You said you had no reason to mistrust her, but it seems as if you're obviously looking for reasons. Ease your suspicion by talking to your girlfriend about your concerns.

Leena
It's all way too fishy. Trust your instinct. She quickly closed out of her email, and you've suspected something all along. Now, the evidence has been virtually planted right in front of you. I fear that she may be seeing another man and has plans to continue the affair. If you don't end the relationship now, you're a fool.

Chapter 15: **Trust No One**
Scene: Bathroom Buzz Kill

At 21, I hooked up with a ruggedly cute guy named Mike, who was too much of a partier and someone my parents forbade me to date. In the years that followed, I often ran into him around town, and we'd always flirt and reminisce about our college years.

Ten years later, the wild boy grew up and settled down with a beautiful blonde. I, too, committed to a great man, who ironically turned out to be Mike's friend. I told my boyfriend, Adrian, about my one-night romp with his friend, and he was fine with it. He appreciates the fact that I had a life before him and, as far as he was concerned, he had nothing to worry about.

One night, Adrian and I arrived at a crowded house party where Mike and his girlfriend happened to be. We had been party-hopping, and I was bit tipsy. I needed to check my appearance and headed to the bathroom. On my way, I passed Mike, who gave me a wink and a devilish smile. I looked in the mirror and was dismayed by my image. My darn cheeks gave me away every time I drank, turning all red on me! As I turned on the faucet to cool my cheeks, I heard the doorknob turn and in walked Mike.
"What are you doing in here?" I yelled at him.
He laughed and said, "Just came over to help you wash your hands." He came from behind and wrapped his arms around me in an embrace, grabbed the bar of soap, and seductively lathered my hands with it. I quickly turned around and splashed him in the face.

We were interrupted by a knock on the door and a voice saying, "Hey, hurry up in there! There's a line out here."
Mike blurted, "Okay, okay, I'm coming. Just chill."
A woman sensed the uncomfortable reaction and a familiar voice said, "Mike, are you okay in there? Can I come in?"

Oh my gosh, this is not good, I thought. We hadn't done anything wrong, but I was drunk and knew that it didn't look good. I quickly decided to jump in the bathtub and drew the curtains closed. Mike walked out and said he'd come back to give me a "coast is clear" sign.

So there I was—drunk, flushed, nervous, and squatting in a stranger's bathtub, trying not to take a breath or make a sound while a guy was taking a whiz right in front of me. He left and in came another, and another, and another. It was the only bathroom in the house, and the line was pretty long. I was worried that my boyfriend was looking for me! I surely would look guilty coming out. Did I do anything wrong?

ASK SASS

SASS Takes *__Bathroom Buzz Kill__*

Reham
You did nothing wrong, so get a grip! The booze is making you feel guilty over nothing. Do not blame yourself for his advances, but don't try to cover for him either. Come clean and tell your man about his buddy.

Rana
Do not create anymore drama by telling your partner. When the next partier is done whizzing, prepare your escape. Get out of the tub, walk right past the incoming person with a confident air and poise, and simply say "excuse me." People can get away with almost anything if they carry themselves in a confident manner.

Ruba
Why did you put yourself in that situation? You are seeking attention and want your boyfriend to come looking for you. Is there something missing from your relationship? Your boyfriend acted appropriately when you told him about your past with his friend. Perhaps you wanted him to be a bit jealous and are continuing to try to do so.

Leena
First, you're wrong for letting it get that far. You should have left that bathroom the minute he walked into it. Second, you must have been giving him some signals throughout the night, which led him to believe you were looking for something, or he wouldn't have been so forward. Accept responsibility, knowing you had a part in this. Chalk it up as a lesson learned, and stop behaving in such a manner.

Chapter 16: **Psycho Stalker**
*Scene: *69*

I was sick of doling out twenty bucks to the doormen to hook up access for me and my buddies all night. We hit the usual circuit of night clubs, looking for a good time and some action. Little did I know what the evening would have in store.

Sixty bucks later, I was feeling on top of my game, so I called the waitress over to send the hot chick at the end of the bar a drink. She accepted the flirtini and later walked over to introduce herself. As she sipped her cocktail, I discovered that Michelle recently broke up with her long-term boyfriend. We spent the rest of the evening connecting and decided to ditch our friends to share a 3 a.m. breakfast at the downtown Grill. It was too cool. We exchanged numbers and went our separate ways as the sun rose.

I contemplated calling her when I got home but wanted to maintain my cool. I couldn't stop thinking about her and really wanted to talk. I'd pick up the phone, then hang up a dozen times before dialing. Finally, I let the call go through and was shocked to hear a guy on the other end. I hung up immediately. It must have been the wrong number. I dialed once more, only to hear the same voice. I hung up again. What am I doing? A rush of panic came over me. Why did I hang up? How old am I? Maybe it was her roommate or her brother. I tried to reassure myself and decided to try again later.

The day dragged along, and all I could think about was Michelle and my adolescent hang up calls. 3:00 p.m. came and I picked up the phone and called. Again the same frickin' voice answered, and I slammed down the phone. Damn it! Why was I behaving this way? Who was this guy? But here's when I really freaked! They *69ed me. I was cold, stone busted! I was barraged with a dozen questions inquiring who was calling and why. I kept insisting they had the wrong number and hung up. What do I do now? She's bound to figure out it's me. She has my number!

ASK SASS

SASS takes *69

Reham
You can easily get yourself out of this mess by playing dumb. Just say you thought you were calling someone else, didn't recognize the voice on the other end, and that's why you hung up. Apologize and never repeat such adolescent behavior.

Rana
It's hard enough to find someone you like, so in the beginning of a relationship, you should have enough patience and sense to behave as a gentleman. Your barrage of calls would make any girl run the other way. You've ruined it, you freak!

Ruba
Give your fingers a rest. You need to regain your cool. Wait it out and see if she calls you. If not, walk away with whatever dignity you have left.

Leena
There is no need to lie here. Sure it was childish, but no harm was done. Accept responsibility immediately and explain that you were simply excited and nervous. How can a woman crucify you in giving such an honest, heartfelt explanation? It may even flatter her.

Chapter 16: **Psycho-Stalker**
Scene: Sleeping with the Enemy

Six months ago, when I got engaged to a 37-year-old real estate developer, I was ecstatic. While we were dating, he brought me flowers regularly, took me on shopping sprees, and made several attempts to treat me special. When he proposed to me during an amazing, seven-course dinner in San Diego and gave me a six-carat diamond ring, how could I not accept? I was blown away.

I boasted to all my friends about how I landed the dream man, but it wasn't long before I stopped bragging. Once that ring was on my finger, claiming his property, things started to change. He insisted that I take weekly Italian cooking classes so I could make him the home-cooked meals that his mother made. He pressured me to quit my job, insisting that it made me unhappy, and that I would be better off tending to the house and planning our wedding. The weekly floral arrangements stopped coming, and his suave exterior soon became a bit gruff. A temper, which I never thought existed, also revealed itself. He became obsessed with the cleanliness of the house and insisted that I keep things in order.

One Sunday morning we were lying on the couch sipping coffee and reading the paper. I casually put the Sports section on the floor while I continued to read the Entertainment guide. He blurted out, "You're not going to just leave that there like that are you?"
I told him to calm down and that I would clean it when I was done.
He responded, "Pick that up right now. Your job is to keep this house clean, make my babies, and make my dinner!"
I thought he was joking and took a long, hard look at him before I realized that he was dead serious.

The following weeks revealed more behavior along the same lines. He started going out with his friends more often and expected me to stay home. One night, I wasn't going to take it anymore. The wedding was one month away, and I was seriously stressed. My girlfriends called me up to meet them for dinner. I eagerly accepted. We went out and had a great time. They asked me how excited I was about the wedding. I continued to fake my enthusiasm and masked my worry and true sentiments, for they all envied me, thinking I had caught Mr. Perfect.

A few hours later, I came home to an angry, inquisitive fiancé.

"Where the hell were you?" he demanded. "Who were you with?" he went on. "How dare you leave this house without asking my permission."
I said, "You're possessed and I'm going to bed."
Shortly after, he got in bed with me, turned on his side, grabbed my neck, and said, "If you ever cheat on me, I will have you killed."
I laughed at him and shrugged it off.
He continued, "I mean it doll, you are mine. You will not disrespect me in this town without paying the consequences. You will never leave me!" Then he gave me a long, mean, hard look.
Who was this person?

ASK SASS

SASS Takes *Sleeping with the Enemy*

Reham
I bet those six carats blinded you! Come on, you must have seen this coming. Too many people rush into marriage before really knowing their partner. Sounds like you were too busy fabricating this fantasy in your head, rather than acknowledging the reality in your bed.

Rana
I can see it now; fast forward to two hours later. He rolls over with a pillow in his hand and a mad look in his eyes as he tries to suffocate you. You are fortunate that you haven't committed to him further. His true personality is starting to reveal itself under the pressure. Run as fast as you can before he puts a hit out on you.

Ruba
Tell him you will not tolerate his mood swings or abusive threats anymore. He definitely wants to play the manly role and expects you to be the good, little wife. If you are not prepared to do that, then you need to spell out what you are willing to do. These issues need to be addressed before you make a lifelong commitment.

Leena
This man needs some serious anger management therapy. It's obvious that he doesn't have much respect for you, and perhaps that can be attributed to his upbringing. Encourage him to seek counseling right away—if not for the two of you, then at least for himself.

Chapter 16: **Psycho-Stalker**
Scene: Restraining Order

My business partner's wife, Kim, was a very young, attractive woman with two children. Kim was an idealist, marrying her first love, Miguel, at the young age of eighteen. They grew up together, carving out a traditional family life for themselves.

While Miguel and I were working together in California on our first project, I had the opportunity to meet Kim. Miguel invited me over for a home-cooked meal with his family. Kim was an amazing cook but seemed somewhat modest around me. Miguel and I drank wine, discussed business, lit a couple of cigars, and outlined our forthcoming venture.

Everything was moving along nicely. A couple of months passed and we solidified the game plan for our new company. Miguel put in his notice where he was working and planned on moving back to Philadelphia. In our first two months of business, we had secured several clients but remained understaffed. This presented a predicament because we were running rather tight on funds. Miguel and I would often forgo our weekly compensation and keep the money in the business to pay our staff and bills.

When I arrived to work one morning, I saw Kim sitting in one of our workstations reviewing our checkbook and accounting information. I asked Miguel to meet me in the conference room right away. "What is Kim doing here, and why is she reviewing our books?" I asked.

Miguel said that he and his wife were having some difficulties and that she didn't think we should hire an assistant because we weren't bringing checks home. I told Miguel that Kim needed to leave immediately, but he wouldn't tell her. Thus, I was forced to call Kim into the conference room and question her. She said that there was no reason to hire a secretary because she would perform those duties for the company pro bono. I explained our strict policy on nepotism and clearly stated that she was no exception.

I told her to get her things and leave the hiring of office personnel to Miguel and me. She refused to leave. I was forced to raise my voice and tell her that if she didn't leave I would make a big scene in front of the whole office, which would embarrass her and, ultimately, her husband.

Then she grabbed my hand and said, "Why are you talking to me this way? Don't you know that I really have a soft spot for you?"

Flustered, I tried to collect my thoughts and said, "Kim, please leave and we'll address this office situation some other time." She reluctantly grabbed her purse and walked out the door.

The following week, Kim called me on my cell phone and asked if she could talk to me in person. She insisted that it was urgent. She explained, "The problem is Miguel. I think he's depressed, and he has been drinking almost every night."
I told her I would meet her in an hour. Now, my brain was in overdrive. My partner might be having a nervous breakdown. He apparently had a drinking problem due to the pressure of our new business. What was I going to do? I cancelled my meetings and headed toward the restaurant.

When I arrived, Kim was already seated in a secluded part of the restaurant. She stood up and gave me a tight hug—and a seemingly slow, lingering kiss on the cheek. I was a little stunned, considering that I almost chased her out of the office the previous week. I rationalized that she was just thankful I took the time to meet with her to discuss her husband. "So, what exactly is going on?" I asked her.
She replied that our conversation must remain confidential.
I said, "Listen, I am sitting here with my business partner's wife at a restaurant in the middle of the day. I cancelled two

meetings to get here, so you're damn right this must remain confidential!"

Kim told me she kicked Miguel out of the house a couple of days ago and that he was taking it pretty hard. She said she needed a break because she was interested in someone else. No wonder the poor guy had been drinking.

Kim then looked at me, grabbed my hand, and asked if I knew the real reason she came to my office last week. I didn't dare say a word. With a provocative look, she confessed she came to the office to get my attention because she had been thinking about me since California.

She went on to say, "I have not been with any other man in my life except Miguel, but the feelings I have for you cannot be denied."

I quickly slid my hand away from hers and told her that, even though I was flattered, she was probably just a little confused.

She replied, "I have been waiting for so long to tell you my feelings."

Now, this was an amazingly attractive woman, who was obviously on fire and wanted to have an affair with me. For a split second, I was both excited and freaked out. I wasn't seriously seeing anyone, and the possibility was enticing, except for two major issues— Miguel and our business. I told her it could never work between us. But Kim kept challenging my logic, telling me that she no longer lived with Miguel and just wanted to go out on one date with me. I told her that, out of respect for Miguel, I had to decline. She asked me to just think about it. I excused myself, telling her I had to attend a meeting.

Two nights later, my home phone rang. It was Miguel's cell number on the caller ID. I grabbed the phone, "Hey, Miguel." Then I heard her voice. It was Kim telling me that she was in my neighborhood. She wanted to know if she could come over

for a glass of wine and talk about what had happened. I told her I was busy and that I was getting ready to leave shortly.
Kim aggressively said, "Stop lying. I just passed by your house 10 minutes ago and saw you through the window. You're wearing shorts and you probably have no plans."
My heart jumped. I told her I'd call her back, and I hung up before she could say another word. I ran to the front of the house and started lowering the blinds while simultaneously turning off all the lights. When I got to the last window, I saw Kim's minivan coming down the street.

I couldn't believe this was happening to me. I was petrified of a hot woman on the prowl. My phone rang again, and it was the same number. I decided not to answer. At the same time, headlights flashed onto the front of my house, and I was sure Kim just pulled into my driveway. What was I going to do?

I got on my hands and knees and crawled to the hallway closet. This was my business partner's wife; this was crazy. My heart was pounding through my chest. I heard a bang on the front door.

"It's Kim! Please, let me in. I have to talk to you."

This went on for a few minutes. Meanwhile, I was hiding like some little girl in a horror movie with a monster on the chase. Kim made one last attempt by opening the mail chute and yelling my name.

She kept saying, "I know you're in there! Stop trying to be so noble."
How do I get myself out of this one?

ASK SASS

SASS Takes *__Restraining Order__*

Reham
Before Missy starts boiling bunnies in your kitchen, I suggest you confront her head on. Stop hiding in the closet like a wimp; invite her in and resolve this obsession once and for all.

Rana
There are several avenues to take here, but they are all pretty messy, so I would opt for the easiest. Tell your business partner, and let him handle the situation. I've had several stalkers, and I hate confronting them. There is something very disturbing about it. Avoid the confrontation and let someone else handle it.

Ruba
She's obviously going through some emotional turmoil and probably has no one else to turn to. She has never been with anyone except her husband, from whom she is currently estranged. Be a bit more compassionate, and allow her the opportunity to speak with you as an adult, instead of hiding in your closet.

Leena
How can you sisters say "act like an adult" and "quit acting like a wimp?" He has told her that he doesn't want to be with her and she has turned completely psychotic! I don't blame him for hiding. You need to continue to avoid her. If you do so, in time, she'll come to realize she's not desired and will stop her mad manhunt.

Chapter 17: **Next Step**
Scene: Hostile Take Over

I asked my girlfriend to move in with me about a month ago. I really love her and thought we were ready for the next step. Before I made the "big" commitment, I thought it would be a good idea to try and live together. She was extremely excited at the opportunity to play homemaker. In fact, she jumped all over it and moved into my place within three days.

"Do you want to think it over for a while?" I asked her.

She was excited to stay with me and saw no reason to wait. At least this was an opportunity for me to see how compatible we would be as husband and wife.

I was having second thoughts. After one week as roomies, she had rearranged just about every room in the house. She turned it into a pink, scented palace. First, she posted a running list on the refrigerator, reminding me of things to do. Then she started incessantly cleaning the house, waking me every morning with the annoying sound of the vacuum cleaner. Gone were my sports magazines. Gone were the posters I had hanging on the walls. Gone was my foosball table. They all magically disappeared, without a trace—and certainly without consulting me first! As replacements, I had new fruit and vegetable still life portraits adorning the walls, silk flower arrangements atop every coffee table, and candles everywhere! There are even his/hers monogrammed towels in my bathroom. How did all this happen so fast?

Today was the topper! As I approached my house after work, I noticed three bags of garbage on the front porch. I knew it wasn't trash day, so I was a little curious to see what was inside. I rummaged through the bags, and I could not believe my discovery. There, before me, were my favorite sports t-shirts, college sweatshirts, and jeans, along with many other cherished articles of clothing, all crumbled up in wrinkled balls. Who is she to give away my possessions without my consent?

ASK SASS

SASS Takes *__Hostile Take Over__*

Reham
The best way to resolve this issue fairly is to divide the house up into rooms, and don't forget that the garage counts. Each of you will get to decorate your areas in your own style.

Rana
I am sorry men, but just please steer clear of any and all decorating issues—very few of you know how to do it right. It's the woman's job; let her do it. You have no business hanging up such gaudy, five-and-dime mall merchandise items, such as posters and sporting memorabilia. Trust her judgment. This is a woman's area of expertise.

Ruba
I think the real reason you are freaking out is that she is living with you, and you may have committed too soon to such a major decision. It sounds like you were hoping that she'd think about it before actually making the move. Take a step back, and look at your real feelings about her. This isn't about the decorating.

Leena
Who does she think she is? Only a week and she owns the place? That was unfair of her to take the liberty of rearranging your belongings and disregarding your possessions without your consent. Establish some basic rules or guidelines because she has really overstepped her boundaries.

Chapter 17: **Next Step**
Scene: So Now What?

I've been in the same sweats for four days now. I haven't showered. I've barely eaten and I won't pick up the phone. Thank God I'm done with law school and have my summer off to deal with this nightmare. I mope around all day on the couch with my box of Kleenex, watching soap operas and bursting into tears every fifteen minutes. My friends are concerned. They haven't stopped phoning. The machine picks up their calls. "Amy, I'm worried about you. Please call me." "Amy, where are you? I know you're there, pick up." "Amy, please talk to me." They are all so sweet to be concerned, but I have to get through this on my own. I'm so embarrassed. How could I even face them anyway?

James and I recently broke up. We were together for five years and were soon to be engaged— that is, until his double life was exposed. We were dating long-distance while I finished law school in New York. He was back home in Chicago. I suppose it was my fault really. I should have picked up on the signs long ago. In retrospect, there were so many. Was I in denial? Was I desperate? What made me stick with him for so long with so much uncertainty?

The summer before last, the evidence was surfacing. I'd call James' house to speak with him and his roommates would often answer the phone. From time to time, they would mistakenly greet me as Eva. Initially, I didn't think anything of it. On other occasions, I'd notice their discomfort when I inquired, "Who's Eva?" When I confronted James, he brushed it off saying that Eva was a friend of his from work. I didn't make too much of it.

Six months ago, James came to New York to visit me during the holidays. He stayed for five days, three of which he received late-night phone calls on his cell. He never bothered to answer in my presence. Again, I didn't make too much of it.

We were having a wonderful weekend, and it was so nice to be together after two months apart. We left that weekend with plans to see each other again the next month.

A few weeks ago, I finished my last term and excitingly prepared for James' visit. We planned a get-away weekend to the Hamptons with some of our friends, which I was looking so forward to. I kept thinking this was the perfect opportunity for James to propose. I was sure he had the ring, since we already talked about possibly getting married next New Year's.

I picked James up at the airport, and we headed to the Hamptons to meet our friends. When we finally arrived, we eagerly settled in and caught up with everyone. That night we decided to head out to one of the local pubs for some drinks.

We were at the bar ordering a round of drinks when this girl tapped James on the shoulder. "Aren't you Eva's boyfriend from Chicago?" she asked. I thought I surely must have misheard what she had just said. James quickly turned around and pretended he didn't hear her. She tapped him once again and said, "James, right?" He faked being preoccupied at the bar by trying to get the bartender's attention to order drinks.

I felt faint; my entire body went numb. I had heard the name Eva several times before. It couldn't be. Were my worst fears coming true? I tried to tell myself there had to be some explanation. I quickly grabbed the girl by her arm and escorted her to the ladies' room. I noticed James looking nervously in our direction. Once inside, I bombarded the girl with questions about Eva, only to discover what I had always feared. James had cheated on me. Not once, not twice, but for two years with Eva, a girl from his office. They were "boyfriend and girlfriend." I was devastated! How could this happen?

ASK SASS

SASS Takes *__So Now What?__*

Reham
I'm sorry, but are you the most clueless woman in the world? What were you waiting for, a smack upside the head? His roommates called you by the other woman's name. He gets late-night phone calls, which he doesn't pick up in your presence. What else are you not telling us? Come on, there's no way you didn't see it coming. You only hurt yourself when you look the other way.

Rana
Woman, count your blessings that this didn't happen three years into the marriage, when kids may have been involved! As hard as it may seem now, you were very fortunate to have found out when you did. Be angry, be sad, just don't remain his girlfriend.

Ruba
For a lot of us, when we go through a break up, we experience a loss of a loved one. You are going to go through five stages of grief: denial, anger, bargaining, depression, and acceptance. Learning about the natural and expected order of emotions will assist you through your recovery and healing process.

Leena
Perhaps people treat you the way you allow them to. You knew from the get-go that things didn't add up, and you continued to ignore the situation. You have to work on your self-esteem so this does not happen to you again.

Chapter 18: **Tying the Knot or Not?**
Scene: Venezuelan Vixen in Vegas

I'm with my two best friends on the beach in Costa Rica. It's hot, it's beautiful, and it's my second week here. It's been a lot of fun, but I'm ready to go home. We have five days left, and we've done just about everything.

I am trying to find a shady spot on the beach to read my book when I look up and see this amazingly beautiful woman. She is a tanned goddess wearing a thong string bikini. She has long, dark, wavy hair, and her body is just rocking. I don't speak Spanish very well, and frankly, I am tired of trying to communicate with the women down here. Between my Spanish 101 and their broken English, it's been frustrating, to say the least. I continue to read my book and watch her walk away.

The next day, I'm at the beach again, and who comes by in a thong bikini and riding a white horse, but my tanned goddess. The horse is galloping, her hair is swaying behind her, and the water is splashing on her long beautiful legs. It's just ridiculous—right out of a movie. Why is this woman taunting me? She rides off with the sun on her back.

Day three, on the beach, same place, and there she is again, this time talking to a group of guys, and I cannot believe my ears. She is speaking English! Without a moment's hesitation, I walk up and introduce myself. Turns out she is Venezuelan, lives in France, and speaks English with a cute French accent. Now mind you, I am a skinny white guy with no striking features, and she is talking to three handsome, tanned volleyball players. But all my insecurities vanish when she gives me her undivided attention. She suggests we take a hike to a hidden lagoon. I eagerly agree. She straps on her backpack and hiking sandals, and we take off.

An hour and a half into our arduous hike, she's stripped down to that thong string bikini. This makes it hard for me to appreciate the astounding wildlife we encounter along the path. There are huge spiders, snakes, monkeys, and tons of other exotic animals. Finally, we arrive at the lagoon. She pulls out two bottles of wine and some French bread, and I pull out some protein bars. We eat, we swim naked, and we make love. And I'm thinking this cannot really be happening to me.

We spend two days at the retreat, our food has run out, and I'm supposed to leave tomorrow. We hike back into town, and she says in her cute little accent, "Give me your ticket." I hand over my airline ticket. She comes back and says, "You stay for two more weeks with me."
I explain that I can't. I have to get back to work.
She says, "Give me your employer's number?"
I oblige.
She comes back and says, "I tell your boss that you come home in two weeks."
I can't believe it. We're with each other for two amazing weeks, and we decide that we are going to get married.
She goes back to Paris and I go home. We agree to get married in Las Vegas a week later. She says she's always wanted to get married among the lights and glitter. I come home and tell all my friends and family the good news. They are shocked, but I don't care, I'm glowing. This is amazing. For one week, we call and email each other constantly. I count the days, and even the minutes, before I see her again.

Finally, the day is here! I rush off to the airport to get her. We embrace and kiss each other all over. We're walking through the airport, and she asks me who I've told about our plans.

"Everyone!" I say excitedly.
"You tell your ex-girlfriends?" she asks me.
"Well no, not really, just friends and family," I reply.

We get to the car and start our road trip. We drive for about 10 hours and get to Nebraska, where we stop to rest and spend the night with some of my friends. The previous hours were interesting to say the least. She asked me all about my exes. Questions like: how pretty were they, how often do I see or talk to them, who was prettier, and many more questions along the same lines. I assured her she had nothing to worry about. Once the questioning about the exes stopped, she started accusing me of looking at other women who passed by while driving on the freeway.

"Why are you looking at her?" she'd accuse. "Do you know that woman? She looked at you when we passed."

Finally, we get to Jason and Kelly's house. After enjoying a wonderful dinner with them, they show us to the guestroom to rest up for our early morning departure. Behind closed doors, the interrogation starts up again.
"Why were they flirting with you?" she asks.
"Who the hell are you talking about?" I yell. I'm too tired to believe this line of questioning. I tell her that she's nuts and she has nothing to worry about. She's convinced that they BOTH like me and that BOTH Jason and Kelly want to sleep with me. She makes us leave at midnight. I apologize to my bewildered friends, and too exhausted to fight or drive, we spend an uncomfortable night in the car. I doze off with her nagging in my ear.

We head back out on the road when the blaring sun wakes us at 6 a.m. I am barely awake, gulping down my gas station coffee, when she starts with her crazy line of questioning again.

"Why was the gas lady looking at you like that?"

We drive for three more hours.

"Who's that girl in the white truck?"

My hands are clenched tightly around the steering wheel. We make it halfway into Colorado before I start thinking that maybe I should turn the car around and head home. Should I?

ASK SASS

SASS takes *<u>Venezuelan Vixen in Vegas</u>*

Reham
Marriage is a huge commitment—one you shouldn't take so whimsically. I'll excuse you because I'm sure visions of her in that thong on a white horse must have temporarily blinded you. Either that or those two days of sun at the lagoon gave you dementia. Put the engagement on hold for now.

Rana
She's one hot-blooded mama, that's for sure. If you marry this woman, she is going to have you locked up in solitary confinement. I'm sure she's probably the hottest and most passionate woman you've had, but think with your head and not your "man tool." So many marriages end in divorce because people want to believe in love so bad. Assess whether you can live like this, and come on, I can tell you that you can't. As the saying goes, "If it's too good to be true, then it is." You shouldn't have acted so quickly on this immediate crush. Turn the car around and send her back home.

Ruba
She's on your turf, and you are no longer in vacation mode. Perhaps you are behaving differently, sending out warning signals. Maybe your actions are causing her insecure behavior. We should always take a look at ourselves first to see if we are the cause of an action. Do this before making any final decisions.

Leena
Did you ever consider that maybe she, too, was swept off her feet? There may be a sense that this is all too good to be true, and she's just waiting for something to go wrong. You need to continually reassure her of your feelings. In doing so, her insecurities will diminish.

Chapter 18: **Tying the Knot or Not?**
Scene: Ready Freddy?

"A piece of paper now determines how much I love you? What difference is getting married going to make anyhow? It's all just a big show." Those are the wise words of the man I have been dating for six years. Do you think we will ever get married?

My family and friends have just about had it. They constantly bombard me with questions about when he will commit. Every time I see them, they corner me and start the inquisition about my relationship with my boyfriend. They have become so annoying with their interrogations that I cannot stand to be around them anymore.

My boyfriend and I live together, share a bank account, and have all the same friends. His friends already refer to me as his "wife," and he clearly does not correct them. That makes me believe that he is not completely against getting hitched, but who knows, guys are strange.

I have always wanted to get married and have kids. When I started to date Fred, I knew, right away, that I wanted to marry him. What I didn't know was that Fred was afraid of commitment. Not commitment in the typical sense. He was a committed boyfriend and partner, with not so much as even a glance at another woman. But Fred was afraid of the institution, practically cringing at the word "marriage." Maybe he thought our entire relationship would change once I had a ring on my finger. I don't really understand.

Recently, however, he is much better at discussing the issue. At least he doesn't get up and walk away anymore. But the conversation still seems to go nowhere. He always leaves me with his famous last words, "It's coming soon." Then he gives me the runaround and goes through a list of excuses or one of his diversionary tactics. Can I really sit around and wait for Freddy to be ready?

ASK SASS

SASS takes ## *Ready Freddy?*

Reham
Give Freddy a deadline. Until there's a fire placed under his butt, Freddy's not going to be ready. He can't expect you to wait around indefinitely, so put a timetable on his indecisiveness. Maybe then he'll finally step up to his commitment.

Rana
Girls, if you ever find yourself in this predicament, get out, get out, get out! Six years is way too long. I made the mistake of staying in a relationship for several years. If your goal is to get married and have a family, then the point of dating is to find the person you're going to marry. If you're both not ready after a year or two, kindly say good-bye.

Ruba
He obviously has a huge fear of commitment. What was his childhood like? Were his parents divorced? Or were they unhappily married? Exploring these answers may help you figure out why he is such a commitment phobe. Discuss your concerns and his fears. Your future together cannot be successful until he has resolved these issues.

Leena
If he treats you well and you are happy together, be patient. You cannot pressure someone into a huge commitment. If he's not ready, he's not ready, and nothing you do will make it better. It's like trying to get people to quit smoking if they themselves aren't ready to do so. All of his heart has to be in it or it won't work.

Biographies

Reham

Prior to having two high-spirited young sons, Reham enjoyed a professional career in the advertising industry as an international account executive subsequent to working as an educator. This University of Michigan graduate is currently a freelance corporate consultant providing comprehensive marketing services. In her spare time, she enjoys photography, cooking, interior design and collecting art. As the eldest of six children, Reham became the natural leader and mediator among her siblings, the same approach she often takes in giving out advice.

Rana

Rana is the Media and Public Relations Director for one of Michigan's top tourist attractions. She serves on several cultural arts boards, planning and promoting charitable events throughout the community. Rana has more than ten years experience in the communications field and established her own marketing and PR firm called, The Detroit Marketing Group. She has a Bachelors degree in Public Relations and an MBA in Marketing and Management. In her free time, Rana enjoys tennis, biking and roller-blading. Her high spirit and sense of adventure have taken her ski-diving and on trips around the world including favorites, the Dead Sea and a Kenyan safari. Rana's cut to the chase attitude and philosophy on life is reflected in her advice which is straight and direct, firmly stating who is right or wrong.

Ruba

Ruba is an educator with a Masters degree in Instructional Technology. In addition to her work as a teacher, Ruba is also part-time model. One of Ruba's great passions is experiencing different cultures, leading her to exotic travel destinations throughout the world. Her temperament and life experiences have equipped her with the knowledge and patience to assist in a diverse array of situations. She has a strong intuitive nature and excels at peeling away at the surface until the underlying problem has revealed itself.

Leena

Leena is a children's speech language pathologist with a Bachelors degree in Education and a Masters degree in Speech Therapy. Her commitment to helping children in several capacities is rivaled by her enthusiasm for her career. She is also a freelance model, having worked in print, television, and runway across the United States. In her free time, she enjoys creative home projects, oil painting, and snow boarding. Leena combines a grounded sense of tradition with a modern passion for life, exuding an irresistible energy and outlook.